Front cover: 1887 sketch of Little Unqua
Mansion. Torn down in 1963.

Back cover: Marjorie Post Park. Opened in
1965 on the site of Little Unqua.

Dana,

Enjoy.

George

(Longtime friend of your
Grandmother).

FROM MANSIONS
TO SUBURBIA
THE MASSAPEQUAS
1945 - 1985

GEORGE KIRCHMANN

authorHOUSE®

AuthorHouse™
1663 Liberty Drive
Bloomington, IN 47403
www.authorhouse.com
Phone: 1 (800) 839-8640

Published by AuthorHouse 01/18/2019

ISBN: 978-1-5462-7197-0 (sc)
ISBN: 978-1-5462-7198-7 (e)

Print information available on the last page.

This book is printed on acid-free paper.

CONTENTS

ACKNOWLEDGEMENTS

The idea for this book came from an informal discussion among Trustees of the Historical Society of the Massapequas, many of whom had grown up in the area and lamented the fact that their contemporaries had moved away or had passed away. How could their memories of growing up in the Massapequas be saved? It was spurred on by my awareness of the enormous changes that occurred in American society after World War II. Most people are aware of them, but may not know the details and the sequence of activities. I decided to take on the challenge of documenting and explaining the growth of this locale in the forty years since the war's end.

My first thanks go to the Trustees who sparked my interest in this period of history. Several other Historical Society members were instrumental in providing information and advice. Bill Colfer, Massapequa Park Village Administrator for many years and currently Commander of the Massapequa Park Veterans of Foreign Wars post, knows more about this history than anybody else. He gave several lectures through the School District's Adult Education Program, ranging from the days when Native Americans lived here to the present. He was unfailingly patient and helpful in pointing out gaps in my knowledge and guiding me to valuable sources. Lillian Bryson, whose family has lived here for six generations, was always generous of her time and information, guiding me through her house, which is a treasure trove of artifacts from long ago, and through the Floyd-Jones Servants' Cottage. Her husband Gene, who sadly passed away in 2017, was also helpful, especially regarding the Fire Department and Old Grace Church. Don Nobile provided valuable information about the school system and the teachers' union. Chuck

Mackie, current Historical Society President, has offered unwavering support and encouragement.

The files of the Historical Society were important sources of information, several going back to the early 1800s. The Floyd-Jones Library is another valuable source, with maps and files of local sources, and with a full set of writings and albums by and about the Jones and Floyd-Jones families. The Library also contains an outstanding set of genealogical charts that provide insight into the Jones family up to 1800 and the Floyd-Joneses to the present. Thomas Floyd-Jones sent updated charts from his home in Alabama that bring family records to 2007. The records at the Long Island Studies Institute, located at Hofstra University, were also very worthwhile. Files at the Plainedge Public Library illuminated the area in North Massapequa that was a farming district for almost one hundred years. The Massapequa Public Library shed light on its own history, as well as the entire area. I am deeply grateful to Lee Gundel, who guided me through the maze of on-line information the Library now possesses.

I spared my four children from listening to me talk extensively about Massapequa's history, but they listened patiently when I discussed it and offered helpful questions. My wife Valerie read several drafts and provided insightful comments. She also endured my seemingly endless discussions of events that are documented here and encouraged me to press on when I seemed to hit dead ends. I am eternally grateful to her for her love and support.

I've tried to verify all information in this book either through primary documents or through more than one source. Any omissions or errors are entirely mine. I hope this volume will spur discussions, reminiscences, offers of source material and and follow-up questions that might prompt further research and writing.

Please note that all images in this book are provided courtesy of the Historical Society of the Massapequas, unless noted otherwise.

I. INTRODUCTION: 1945

World War II was over and many veterans were eager to start new lives. This might mean marriage, children, or a resumption of their family situations. For many in the New York area, it also meant moving out of New York City into areas that came to be known as suburbs. Long Island was the best known and the one that is often cited as a textbook example of suburbanization. For men who had fought in the war, New York City came to represent an outdated way of living. Many of them had fought with soldiers from the South, Midwest, or West Coast, and learned about living in private houses, with backyards, trees, gardens, and minimal traffic - areas that required a quick car ride rather than a tedious subway or bus ride to get to work or to home. For those who lived in the four populous boroughs, Jones Beach offered a taste of what life could be like outside New York City and could be reached by pleasantly landscaped parkways.

Levittown was the first large-scale suburban community to spring up, created in the middle of the large, flat and unpopulated Hempstead Plains. It featured private houses priced very cheaply, from $5,000, payable through GI loans. It offered convenient shopping (at one of the four shopping centers created in each of Levittown's four quadrants), schools, playgrounds and neighborliness, through one of the community centers in each quadrant. Shamefully, this neighborliness was racially defined, through the restrictive covenants added by the Levitt Brothers to each mortgage contract in order to keep blacks from moving into the community. It seemed acceptable for blacks to fight alongside whites (and President Truman had integrated the armed forces in 1948), but not to live alongside them. The Supreme Court declared restrictive covenants unconstitutional in 1948, but

1

the Levitts continued to sell only to whites. By 1960 the community was still entirely white, divided almost equally among Jews, Roman Catholics and Protestants.

Veterans who might have wanted housing larger than Levittown's, or who were interested in an already existing community, looked further east and found an area on the Nassau County border that appeared full of positive possibilities. The Massapequas were one of the last Long Island communities settled by whites in the seventeenth century (in 1696), and they had an unusual history centered around the Jones and Floyd-Jones families. Any veteran who thought of buying a home in the area would probably have driven out via the Southern State Parkway, familiar as the route to Jones Beach, and would have encountered unique sections. In the northwest, just south of the Hicksville Road exit of the Parkway, he would have driven through a thriving farming district, populated by mostly German settlers in the 1870s who produced a variety of produce and flowers for the New York market. These farms were small and were worked by families who doubtless worried about the future as they saw settlers moving into new houses.

Just south of the farm district, for example, was an area filled by about one hundred houses, many dating back to the first decade of the twentieth century. These were the results of a building project overseen by the Queens Land and Title Company, which had marked out large sections of the western Massapequas for a proposed new city of 15,000 residents, linked to New York City by the Southern Railroad (later the LIRR Babylon branch). Several dozen houses were built down to Merrick Road, south of which stood more houses, typically small cottages which New York City residents built as summer residences, to escape from the city's heat and overcrowding.

If our prospecting veteran looked east of Hicksville and Merrick Roads, past the golf course that had stood for half a century, he would see about two dozen ornate Spanish-style stone houses, built by William Fox and Joseph Frankel, to entice movie stars and other personalities to settle along the south shore. This development became known as Biltmore Shores. A little further east, the Harbor Green development was created in the early 1930s on land purchased from

2

Fox by the Harmon National Real Estate Corporation. Small houses were built on large 100 by 100 foot lots, without cellars or sidewalks, to cut costs and attract the few customers who were able to purchase houses during the depression. Harbor Green was just south of Grace Church, an 1844 building that was the Floyd-Jones family church and the oldest public building in the Massapequas.

Grace Church and Wylie Hall

There were very few houses north of the church until a driver reached Sunrise Highway, where several dozen houses were built in the twenties by Sears Roebuck and a few dozen more by the Brady Cryan and Colleran real estate firm, which hoped to populate what they convinced the New York State Legislature to create in 1931 as the Village of Massapequa Park. The depression and BCC's illegal business practices had stalled further development, leaving the area sparsely populated and surrounding an airfield, Fitzmaurice Flying Field, that was little used by 1945.

Moving east and just south of the Southern State Parkway, our veteran would have encountered a few farms, but not much along either side of Carman's Road. This held true as far south as Sunrise Highway because the ground was swampy and difficult to build upon. His decision to settle in the Massapequas, as well as many thousands of others, would eventually lead to the creation of Sunrise Mall, but that would not be until 1973. He may have noticed the remnants of Frank Buck's Zoo, begun in 1934 as a wild animal park, but used as a defense plant during the war. It would soon be reborn as the Massapequa Zoo and Amusement Park, delighting veterans' and other residents' children until 1965.

In southeastern Massapequa there were two old cabins along Oakley Boulevard, remnants of Chin Chin Ranch, a sprawling property built by Fred Stone, a famous Broadway actor who attracted many fellow actors to his home in the 1920s. His large yellow house, like most others, was built overlooking Narraskatuck Creek, one of the many streams and creeks that existed throughout the area. Our veteran may have learned that Massapequa was an old Native American term that meant "Place of Many Waters" or "Great Water Land," and that made building houses an unusual challenge. Nevertheless, he and many other veterans were attracted to the houses that sprang up from the late 1940s throughout the entire area. Large sections north of the Oyster Bay water line were filled in with dirt dredged from the Bay, creating several dozen new streets in the 1950s and 1960s. In the next forty years, there was scarcely a piece of land that was not filled with private houses.

A GEOGRAPHY NOTE

The term "The Massapequas" refers to the area south of the Southern State Parkway, east of Tackapausha Preserve, west of County Line Road and north of Jones Beach and Tobay Beach. It consists of the incorporated Village of Massapequa Park in the center, the area known as East Massapequa east of Unqua Road, the area known as North Massapequa north of Jerusalem Avenue and the rest of the area known simply as Massapequa. The Village is the only recognized political entity. The rest of the area consists of communities that have the above informal names. Residents in each of these areas insist upon using these names. An East Massapequan will distinguish himself/herself from a North Massapequan, and those who live in Massapequa Park will emphasize they live in "the Park."

The Village of Massapequa Park, in fact, is probably the best example of the extraordinary post-war growth, from 488 residents in 1940 to 19,904 in 1960. The history of its Village Hall shows how the population growth forced significant changes. From its founding in 1931, Village leadership had used the Schaefer Homestead on Front Street, built in the 1890s for the German population that lived in or visited the area. Population growth forced the destruction of this old and charming building, and a new red brick structure was completed in 1966 to serve Village residents.

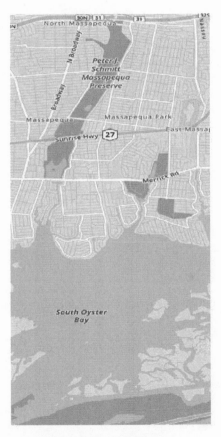

The Massapequas
(Courtesy of Mapquest)

II. Hinting at History: Massapequa's Historic Complex

Massapequa's Historic Complex provides an excellent entrée to a study of its recent history. Its three buildings, located on the north side of Merrick Road opposite Cedar Shore Drive, exist at that location in large part because of the changes that took place in the post-war period. Old Grace Church, built in 1844, became "old" after a new church was built across Merrick Road in 1962 to accommodate the growing Episcopalian presence in the area. The Floyd-Jones Servants' Cottage, from 1870, was moved to its present location because of the interest of its new owners to build a house on the site. Lastly, the Floyd-Jones Free Library, erected in 1896, changed its character and its impact on the Massapequas because of the explosive growth of the school-age population after 1945.

Massapequa's Historic Complex

Old Grace Church

The oldest church in the Massapequas (1844), and for many years the only one, Grace Church, built by the Floyd-Jones family and capable of accommodating 100 worshippers, gradually became too small for the growing Episcopal population that moved into the Massapequas. The building of the new church and the questions surrounding the old church's status were direct results of the enormous growth after World War II. Episcopal Church records show 520 communicants in 1950 and 1,709 in 1960. Old Grace was clearly inadequate to meet the needs of new parishioners. Jones and Floyd-Jones family members had moved from the Massapequas by the end of World War II. Their family church, which gradually fell into disuse, could also have been removed from the scene.

In 1962 a larger church was completed across Merrick Road and services were held there. Old Grace, as it came to be known, was used less and less and suffered from two acts of vandalism (1969) and, in 1981, by the possibility that it might be torn down. The Vestry members of new Grace Church were unwilling to continue paying for an unused and deteriorating building and discussed several possibilities, including its removal. Members of the Massapequa Historical Society, formed in 1969 in response to the vandalism, banded together and recruited several hundred supporters to resist the church's destruction. Their efforts led to the conclusion of a twenty-five year lease, whereby the Society agreed for $10 to take on the maintenance and guardianship of the historic building. These are two direct results of the explosive growth after World War II.

Floyd-Jones Servants' Cottage

Massapequa was the home of wealthy Jones and Floyd-Jones family members for over two centuries, beginning with Tryon Hall (later Fort Neck House) in 1770. Their mansions, which dotted

Merrick Road, became anachronistic by the mid 1900s. The Fort
Neck House as well as the Elbert Floyd-Jones House were destroyed
before the war, and the others came down after it, replaced by private
houses or, in one striking instance, by a large and popular public
park. Family members who lived in the Massapequas for many years
passed away. Their descendants sold their large and expensive estates
to developers who erected hundreds of homes for the new residents,
most of them veterans from Brooklyn and Queens. They were eager
to use their GI Bill money to move to the suburbs.

By the early 1980s, there was one rather modest Floyd-Jones
house and two servants' cottages remaining. One of the latter was
slated for demolition by its owners, until the Historical Society, flush
from saving the church, asked them to wait until they could raise
money to move it from its site near Harbor Lane south of Merrick
Road. The Society secured the funding by 1985 and contracted with
Davis Housemoving to relocate the building across Merrick Road
and reset it on property adjacent to Old Grace Church. It became the
Floyd-Jones Servants' Cottage, and was repurposed as a reminder
of how Massapequans lived many years ago. From being the center
of Massapequa's life, the Jones and Floyd-Jones families became
historical footnotes by 1985.

*Floyd-Jones Servants' Cottage
Moved across Merrick Road*

Floyd-Jones Free Library

The only Library in southeastern Nassau County since its founding in 1896, the Delancey Floyd-Jones Library became the focus of intense and heated discussions in the early 1950s. As the population grew and schools were opened, the need for library services became acute. The small building on Merrick Road across from Cedar Shore Drive, created by Colonel Delancey Floyd-Jones in 1896 for the then sparsely populated area, was clearly too small to meet the needs of the growing population and to hold the many books and related material that students and adult residents would need. The Library Trustees were, for many years, Jones or Floyd-Jones family members and active worshippers at Grace Church. Most School District Board members were newer residents and considered the little building anachronistic. The issue was whether to integrate it into an enlarged library system, or leave it to operate separately. Because it had its own endowment, established by Delancey Floyd-Jones, the New York Secretary of State indicated it would be difficult, expensive and time-consuming to integrate it with the newly-created Central Avenue Public Library.

The Library Trustees were of the same mind and decided to keep the Library open as a separate community-based locale. They continued this tactic for about thirty years, until the larger two-site public system made it essentially irrelevant. Trustees by the mid 1980s repurposed the Library as a historic building. Tellingly, the last Floyd-Jones family member involved with it, Louisa Bonner, had resigned as a Trustee in 1985, citing her age and the inconvenience of traveling from her residence in Manhattan, thus ending the Floyd-Jones family's involvement and making the Library truly a historic artifact.

Cemeteries

The three cemeteries in the Massapequas also reflect the changes that occurred after World War II. The oldest is the **West Neck**, or **Jones**

Cemetery, located on Merrick Road east of Massapequa Avenue. It was established sometime in the early 1700s and contains the remains of about fifty Jones family members. Many of the headstones are faded because of weathering and many others do not have Jones names because of the intermarriages that occurred in the subsequent 200 years. The most recent headstone shows Julia Wellwood, wife of Samuel Jones, who died in 1931.

All current stones are in the western half of the cemetery. The eastern half is bare except for a few remnants of stones and depressions in the ground. Most if not all remains in that area were moved to the Floyd-Jones Cemetery. There may be additional remains in the eastern half, but there is no conclusive evidence. The cemetery was neglected for many years through the twentieth century because there was no record of ownership. As a result of an agreement with the Town of Oyster Bay, the Historical Society has taken conservatorship of the property.

The **Floyd-Jones Cemetery** stands behind Old Grace Church and was created in 1892 by Floyd-Jones family members to hold the remains of their deceased. Several remains were relocated from the Jones Cemetery and burials have continued at the site. The most recent burial occurred in 2009.

Grace Church created its **Cemetery** in 1892, originally to hold the remains of church leaders, that is, rectors and their families and Vestrymen and their families. The older burials were restricted to the northwest corner of the site and a community hall was built by church members in 1940, named Wiley Hall after long-time Rector William Wiley. It remained until 1962 when the new church opened. Its site and the rest of the property remained fallow until the 1990s when the church began to sell burial sites all around the building. A columbarium was erected in 2007. It is still an active cemetery.

III. The Old Order Changes

Where Have All the Mansions Gone?

The early history of the Massapequas can be written around the many mansions that existed along Merrick Road. Beginning in 1770 and continuing until 1965 the Jones and Floyd-Jones families lived in one of several mansions they built along what was for many years the only through road in this area. Originally known as Kings Highway, the name was changed after the American Revolution to South Country Road and to Merrick Road around 1900.

Two mansions had burned before World War II:

Elbert Floyd-Jones's House (unnamed), 1870, burned 1926;

Fort Neck House (originally Tryon Hall), built 1770 by David Jones, burned 1940.

The others existed in 1945 and all, except one, were gone by 1985. They are, in order of destruction

Massapequa Manor, built in 1837 by David S. Jones, purchased by Corroon family in 1918, burned 1952;

Sedgmore, also known as the Oddie House, built 1860 by Coleman Williams and his wife Sarah Floyd-Jones, purchased by the Oddie family ca 1900, torn down 1960;

Unqua, ca. 1860, built by Henry and Edward Floyd-Jones, last owned by Edward Floyd-Jones, torn down around 1960;

Holland House, built by William Carpender and Ella Floyd-Jones 1870, torn down 1962;

Little Unqua, built 1861 by Edward Floyd-Jones, home of Louise Floyd-Jones Thorn for many years, torn down 1963;

Sewan, George Stanton Floyd-Jones's house, 1870, torn down 1963;

Kaycroft, 1830 in Farmingdale, moved to Massapequa ca 1900 and later remodeled, torn down 1965.

A smaller Floyd-Jones House, built in 1870 across from Old Grace Church was used as the Grace Church Rectory and is still standing.

Grace Church Rectory

The process in every instance was the same. The mansions had aged, the original owners had died and their descendants, or current owners, did not want to pay for their maintenance. Real estate developers were eagerly looking for plots on which to build private houses and there was no significant community opposition to their destruction. The Fort Neck House (1940) and Massapequa Manor

(1952) were unoccupied and burned, raising suspicions that the fires were set deliberately to remove the buildings and use insurance money to build on the sites. No evidence was ever produced to support that idea.

In the case of Massapequa Manor, this magnificent structure had been sold by David Jones to his cousin William Floyd-Jones in 1850. It was inherited by William Robison, who married into the family in 1900 and he, in turn, sold it to the Corroon family in 1918. The Corroons kept it until 1947, when the youngest sibling born there, Jack Corroon, sold it to Harbour Green Development. The house faced Merrick Road and the property included a boathouse on Massapequa Lake, a stable, a windmill, and fields for polo and horseback riding.

Massapequa Manor remained empty for several years after 1947 while the developer waited to secure approvals to demolish the building and build over it and the many surrounding acres to the north and east. The site, across from Massapequa Lake, was highly desirable. A fire, started accidentally by trespassers, consumed the house very quickly in November 1952. The developer subsequently built several dozen houses in the area, on streets named Dover Court, Polo Court, Surrey Road, Cambridge Road and Rugby Road, in deference to the history of the site. The groundskeepers' house was moved in 1952 and still stands on Surrey Road.

Massapequa Manor

Sedgmore lasted for a century until its destruction in 1960, to be replaced by private houses. It was purchased by the Oddie family around 1900 and came to be known as the Oddie House. It sat across from today's St. Rosa of Lima Church and School. Little else is known about it or about Unqua, built by Edward Floyd-Jones and later owned by Henry Floyd-Jones. Built and destroyed around the same dates, Unqua stood on the east side of Merrick Road, looking out at South Oyster Bay upon a field that became John Burns Park.

Holland House was a pleasant wooden structure on the south side of Merrick Road, reached from a circular driveway. It was sold to John VonDerVelde, a restaurateur, in the 1920s. He reopened it as the Wagon Wheel Restaurant, a location that became very popular with residents throughout the south shore. As the 1950s wore on, the newly created Diocese of Rockville Center was looking for a site for a Catholic Grammar School and Church. The Wagon Wheel proved ideal because the owners wanted to retire and the site was quite large, originally filled with gardens and later used as the restaurant's parking lot. The Diocese bought the building in 1957 and erected a school, which they named after St. Rose of Lima. While money was raised for a church, the Wagon Wheel was used as a temporary church, painted white and identified with a cross over the front door. Fund-raising efforts led to the destruction of the original building and its replacement by St. Rose of Lima Church in 1965.

Sewan was owned by George Stanton Floyd-Jones, and is considered the most picturesque of the Massapequa mansions. It was built in 1870 by David Richard Floyd-Jones, a former New York Secretary of State and Lieutenant Governor. His son George lived there until his death in 1941. George Stanton Floyd-Jones was an Officer with the Atlantic Mutual Insurance Company, and was influential in founding All Saints Episcopal Church in Seaford. He married Anita Owen, a Catholic, and converted to her religion. She died in 1940 and he died a year later, but had willed that his house be given to the Sisters of Charity of Amityville. The sisters operated it as a grammar school, a perfectly fitting development because of the need for schools after the war. The public school district held classes in the school from 1948 until 1954 and then bought Sewan from the

14

Sisters, tearing it down and building Massapequa High School on the site. The first graduating class was in 1955 and the school became crowded very quickly, and remained so for many years.

Sewan ca 1940

Kaycroft, easternmost of the Jones/Floyd-Jones family's mansions, was declining at the same time. It was built by Walter Restored Jones and located in Farmingdale in the 1830s. Around 1900 his descendants moved the house to Merrick and Unqua Roads, originally calling it Unqua Lodge. It was renamed Kaycroft by Katherine Jones Whipple, who remodeled it extensively around 1910. It remained occupied by the family until the 1960s, when the owners felt the need to sell it because of its expense. It was torn down and is now the site of Parkview Nursing Home.

There was another mansion, built in 1864 and called the Red House, located on Seaford Avenue, that was demolished in 1964. It was built by James Meinell, a Treasurer of Old Grace Church and close friend of the Floyd-Joneses. It had become a rooming house and was last owned by the Masone family. Like the above listed structures, it represented a different way of life and stood in the way of Massapequa's modernization.

James Meinell was a wealthy New York City theater owner

who built his summer house on Massapequa's western border. He was actively involved with the newly built Grace Church, acting as Treasurer in the 1850s. He died in 1865, shortly after completing the Red House, and his descendants lived there until about 1900, when they sold it to a real estate company, which used it as a hotel, rest stop for travelers going to eastern Long Island, and finally as a rental property. The Masone family was the last to live there, in the 1950s, by which time the wood structure had deteriorated significantly. It became a target for developers, who paid handsomely for the 600 acre site, most of which was soon covered with private houses. The western part was given to Nassau County, which created Tackapausha Preserve.

The Carman homestead, on the corner of Carman's and Merrick Road, was not one of the Jones/Floyd-Jones buildings, but was significant as one of the oldest structures in the Massapequas. It was built sometime in the late 1700s and owned and occupied by the Carman family until the early 1900s. It had been used as a stagecoach stop and post office. The Carmans had built a grist mill, and operated it for one hundred fifty years until it was destroyed when the dam north of it, where Berner Junior High School now stands, broke. Water flooded it as well as a later mill built by Dr. Polk, who owned a mansion to the west of Carmen's Road. The intersection of Carman's Road and Merrick Road was known for many years as Carman's Corner.

In the early 1960s, discussions were held with Nassau County about relocating the homestead to the newly-created Old Bethpage Village. Some County leaders had become concerned about the wanton destruction of older buildings throughout the County and developed plans to move structures to a vacant parcel in Old Bethpage, satisfying the thirst of real estate developers to build private houses while preserving slices of Nassau County's past. As discussions continued, a fire of undetermined origin destroyed the building in 1965, eliminating the one possibility of an example of "Old Massapequa" being made available for a large audience.

The last long - standing mansion highlighted here shows very clearly the issues involved in the rapid development of the Massapequas. Little Unqua (located east of Unqua mansion) was built in 1861 by Edward Floyd-Jones, who was a New York State Senator and Queens County Supervisor, marching to the same political drum as his first cousins David Richard, a Lieutenant Governor, and Elbert, a New York State Assemblyman. Edward built Unqua as well as Little Unqua and lived in both at various times. His daughter Louise was born in Little Unqua in 1867 and inherited the mansion and property when she married Conde Thorn in 1889. Her husband died in 1944 and she remained on her estate until her death in 1961. Toward the end of her life, she became the center of a multi-faceted discussion concerning her property.

There is little detailed information about most of Massapequa's mansions, but we know quite a bit about Little Unqua, thanks to the efforts of former Historical Society Trustee Barbara Fisher, who interviewed John Nolan in the late 1980s. Nolan had worked on the estate as a teenager. He described the house as large, with two sets of porches, one over the other, painted a grayish blue, not as pretentious as some of the other mansions that had existed in the Massapequas. The building faced Merrick Road just west of Unqua Road. There was a circular driveway in front that led in from the Unqua - Merrick corner and exited to the west near Unqua Lake. To the left of the house (facing it) was a formal garden with cedar trees and a variety of flowers and plants. Mr. Nolan indicated there was a gardener's cottage behind the house and a garage to the west. A barn and a stable were situated at the northwest corner, near the lake. A paddock with horses was located toward the rear of the property and a riding track was maintained at the northeast corner. Mr. Nolan worked there in 1957, when Mrs. Thorn was ninety years old. He remembered that she was mentally sharp but fragile, and was cared for by her gardener and her daughter, who apparently managed the estate.

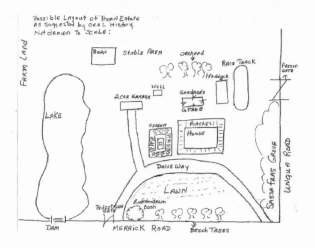

Little Unqua Layout

What Mr. Nolan did not mention, probably because he was too young to appreciate the issue, was the maelstrom that swirled around this prime piece of real estate in the late 1950s. Several suitors were after Little Unqua: the Board of Education wanted to build a school on the northeast part of the property; the Chamber of Commerce was lobbying for a hospital on the site; the Nassau Shores Garden Club felt it was an ideal location for an art museum and cultural center; several real estate developers submitted plans for either private houses, an apartment complex, or a shopping center. All of these proposals were appropriate on their face, but the interested parties had to contend with Mrs. Thorn's occupancy of Little Unqua. She had expressed her disdain at the development of the Massapequas and felt a park of some sort should replace her estate, but only after her death.

Into this difficult situation stepped another notable woman, Marjorie Rankin Post. Born in New Jersey in 1895, she moved with her family to the Massapequas in the early twentieth century. Her father was appointed Postmaster and she succeeded him in 1922, becoming Massapequa's first Postmistress. She subsequently became involved in operating an insurance company, and worked as an ambulance driver in World War II, ferrying wounded soldiers from the Brooklyn Navy Yard to Mitchel Field for treatment. She later became active in local politics and was appointed to a vacant seat on the Town of Oyster Bay's Council in 1957, becoming its first Councilwoman.

Marjorie Post knew Mrs. Thorn through her activities in the Massapequas, and sided with her in her wish to change Little Unqua into a park. Her lobbying paid off after Mrs. Thorn's death in 1961, because Oyster Bay's Town Council voted to purchase the forty-two acre property for $893,000. Subsequent votes approved spending $2.5 million to tear down Little Unqua and construct a park based on the recently-completed Plainview-Bethpage Community Park: three swimming pools, handball and tennis courts, picnic grounds, playgrounds, and ample parking. Upon its completion in 1965, the park was named for Marjorie Post, despite her objections.

Marjorie Post
(Courtesy of the Massapequa Post)

The last "old" building demolished in the Massapequas wasn't a Floyd-Jones house, but it deserves mention because of its history and its inclusion in the list of those that were torn down in the name of progress. The Baldwin-Hilbert House stood on Merrick Road at the corner of County Line Road. It was built in the 1850s and purchased by Timothy Baldwin, a Civil War veteran who lived there with his family until 1910. It subsequently passed into the possession of Dr. Kenneth Hilbert, a veterinarian who was renowned for his knowledge of poultry diseases. He became very busy in the 1930s when Frank Buck's Zoo opened, caring for the many animals there until 1965, when the zoo, operating as Massapequa Kiddie Land, closed. The house was sold by Stuart Hilbert, the doctor's son, to developers who promised to restore it. Through a suspicious set of circumstances, involving supposed miscommunications, the house was torn down in 1998, removing the last remnant of Massapequa's grand estates.

WHERE HAVE THE JONESES/FLOYD-JONESES GONE?

As the mansions disappeared in the 1940-1985 period, their owners moved away too. Most of the Jones family members, direct descendants of Thomas Jones, had moved to the Cold Spring Harbor area in the early 1800s, but many still owned property in the Massapequas. A 1914 map shows that John Jones owned several acres in East Massapequa, but these were sold to several buyers, including the New York Water Company, which sold it in the 1960s to a developer who built Sunrise Mall. Few other Joneses appear to have stayed in the area and their number in the Cold Spring Harbor area dwindled out through intermarriage. The last direct descendant of Thomas Jones was Mary Gardiner Jones, born in Cold Spring Harbor, and later a resident of Washington, D.C., where she held several governmental and private positions. She died in 2010 and is buried in the Memorial Cemetery of St. John's Church in Syosset, as are many of the Joneses.

The Floyd-Jones family members also faded away, along with their property. Henry Floyd-Jones owned a piece of property along County Line Road north of Sunrise Highway until the end of World War II. George Stanton Floyd-Jones, an influential family member and one of the last residents, died in 1941 after willing his estate to the Catholic Sisters of Charity, who ran it as a parochial school until 1954, when it was bought by the School District and used as the site for Massapequa High School. The large site east of the High School was owned by Edward H. Floyd-Jones, who sold what became the

Arlyn Oaks development after the war. Louise Floyd-Jones kept her "Little Unqua" estate until 1963.

One Floyd-Jones descendant lives in Amityville and provides services for the Historic Complex, another resides in Cold Spring Harbor and is the administrator of the Floyd-Jones Cemetery. The others have moved throughout the United States, living in Alabama, Florida and Arizona.

IV. Alterations

Housing

Analysts have identified five characteristics of postwar suburbs, which serve as handy guides for understanding change in the Massapequas.

1. Peripheral location. Vacant land outside cities was filled in, rather than vacant land in cities.
2. Low density. Single family detached dwellings. 10,500 people per square mile, half the density of older suburbs or cities.
3. Architectural similarity. One or two story ranch houses common, without parlor, hall, or porch.
4. Easy availability and reduced suggestion of wealth. Cheaper to build in suburbs than to rebuild in cities.
5. Economic, age and racial homogeneity. "We can solve a housing problem, or we can try to solve a racial problem. But we cannot combine the two." William Levitt.

Returning veterans began to look for private housing immediately after World War II. Interestingly, they were continuing a trend from the 1930s. Despite the depression, many city dwellers had begun to move out to what were then commonly called the suburbs, in search of comfort, convenience, safety and, above all, home ownership. They were helped by several programs created by President Franklin D. Roosevelt and his New Deal Democrats to make housing more affordable to people who might otherwise not be able to afford it. The 1933 Home Owners Loan Corporation was designed to provide affordable loans to home buyers. It gave them thirty years to repay their loans. This represented a momentous change in thinking about home ownership. Before, homes were things that wealthy people could afford and they were expected to pay them off upon purchase or shortly thereafter. For the first time, a prospective buyer could put down very little money and not worry about making large monthly payments. In the first two years of its existence, the HOLC provided $3 billion for over 1,000,000 mortgages, fueling a rush from inner cities.

Helping the process of suburbanization was the automobile, produced in large numbers in the 1920s, largely through Henry Ford's assembly line production techniques. Although car manufacturing slowed significantly in the 30s, many owners clung to their cars and used them as the primary means of transportation when they moved to the suburbs. Thus, while public transportation reigned in cities, especially larger ones, cars, which had been found to clog older cities' streets, would be the primary, and often, the only mode of transportation in suburbs. Robert Moses provided the geographic blueprint with his statewide highway system, creating easy access to all of Long Island via the Southern State Parkway (begun 1927, completed 1962), the Northern State Parkway (1935 - 1965) and the Long Island Expressway (1940 – 1972). The latter ran through the middle of the island and opened it to development on an unprecedented scale.

The Massapequas provide a splendid example of these two developments. Movie producer William Fox had gone bankrupt after the 1929 market crash and Harmon National Bank bought his undeveloped property south of Merrick Road, and continued to build houses in Biltmore Estates. Similarly Harbor Green was defined in 1933, when builders erected small houses on large (100 by 100 foot) lots, using the twin lures of space and privacy to attract buyers. Similar growth, slow though it was, continued in Massapequa north of Sunrise Highway through the Queens Land and Title Company and in Massapequa Park, through successors to Brady Cryan and Colleran. The population of the Massapequas went from 2,000 in 1931 to 3,500 in 1940, and of Oyster Bay from 36,869 to 42,594. More broadly, Nassau County's population grew significantly also:

from 303,053 in 1930 to 406,758 in 1940. But note the postwar jump: to 672,765 by 1950 and 1,225,227 by 1960.

These statistics provide an insight to the rush to the Massapequas after World War II. Once again, the government led the process through passage of the GI Bill and the work of the 1930s Federal Housing Authority. The GI Bill of Rights was designed primarily to ease returning servicemens' reintegration to peacetime society, by providing money to meet their expenses while they sought jobs and money to pay for education and/or training to equip them for well-paying positions. A section of the bill allowed assistance for home buying, but that was not stressed originally, despite a 1943 government report that showed 41% of soldiers planned to buy private houses after the war. Pressed hard by the American Legion, Congress passed the measure to provide subsidies to veterans who returned to school, and loan guarantees to those who wished to purchase homes. In the few years after the war, 4 million eligible veterans purchased homes, using low interest long term loans guaranteed by the federal government.

The immediate beneficiaries of this bill on Long Island were those who purchased homes on the Hempstead Plains, on land bought and developed by the Levitt family, Abraham and his sons William and Alfred. They began in Roslyn, completing 2,250 homes in Roslyn in 1946, in the $17,500 to $23,500 price range. These amounts were far above the means of returning veterans, but the Levitts soon moved south, buying 4,000 acres of potato farms and grassland. They built houses using mass production techniques they had perfected in their first housing development, in Norfolk, Virginia in 1941. They put down concrete slabs, had supplies delivered to the site (they owned the lumber yards and concrete factories), instructed construction crews how and when to complete certain tasks, and minimized costs by banning labor unions. In the period from 1947 to 1950, they completed 17,400 houses, providing living space for 82,000 residents. The average house cost $8,000 and was equipped with kitchen appliances and a TV set. Down payment was typically $400.

Levittown, as it became known, was completed by the beginning of the Korean War, which meant World War II veterans who had returned to the workforce or had used the GI Bill for higher education, had to look elsewhere. They moved east and south in Nassau County, filling up Hicksville, Bethpage, Farmingdale, and older south shore communities such as Freeport, Merrick, Bellmore, Wantagh, Seaford and, eventually, Massapequa. By 1950, there were an estimated 15,000 building lots for sale in this area.

Arlyn Oaks, Merrick Road, 1952

There were many builders in the Massapequas, all offering enticements to veterans of either war to relocate here throughout the 1950s. A house built in 1947 on Forest Avenue south of Sunrise Highway for a long-time resident cost his father $7,000. One built for his aunt the previous year on one of the canals leading to South Oyster Bay had cost $7,500. The area around Beach Road, Forest Avenue, and Linden Street was sparsely developed with a few small and plain houses.

Prices changed as the 1950s brought many prospective homeowners. A review of 13 builders in the early 1950s shows an average down payment of $695 for veterans versus $2,968 for non-veterans. These amounts were for houses costing between $10,750 and $$17,990. The latter were the "Cadillac Houses" built on the former Massapequa Manor estate, overlooking Massapequa Lake. Other models included the Hamilton split level on Park Lane, the Massapequa Shores homes on Division Avenue south of Merrick Road, and Brewster Manor, costing $14,990 and located in northwest Massapequa in the fast-disappearing farming district. Clearly housing costs accelerated in the 50s because of the demand, but purchasing for veterans was easy with little or no down payment required. The Hamilton Split, for example, required no down payment, the Brewster Manor required $990 down, as opposed to the typical 10% to 20% traditional builders had requested. These houses were built on open land, as the 1952 aerial view of Arlyn Oaks, east of the High School, shows.

Interestingly, coal was a cheap and available source of fuel until the 1950s, but most new houses were built with oil burners, because oil was becoming more abundant and easier to deliver. Massapequa Fuel Oil Company, owned for many years by the Beato family, was one of the largest businesses in the locality. Later in the seventies the cost of oil skyrocketed and home and business owners began converting to natural gas. The Beato family retained most of its customers through a combination of good service and personal loyalty.

SCHOOLS

The school system underwent enormous change inevitably, as new homeowners moved in with their young children or had children after they became Massapequans. A hint of change had occurred in 1925, when the Massapequa School was built to replace the small wooden two room schoolhouse that had stood on Park Boulevard for over fifty years. The first "modern" school was made of brick, had four classrooms, a room for the Principal and for the school administration, a kitchen and an auditorium that doubled as a cafeteria. It was expanded in 1930 and again in 1939, but that change was as nothing compared to what happened after 1945. That one school, for example, doubled in size in 1950 through addition of a separate wing and creation of a basement.

Ironically, the original school did not have a basement because the ground was too wet because of the water level. As houses were built north of the school, leading up toward Sunrise Highway, water demands lowered the water level and better construction techniques allowed District 23 to create a basement. The original building held 79 pupils in 1925, but 850 by 1948. Improvements to the first school, renamed **Fairfield**, helped students who lived in the area west of Massapequa Lake and north of Merrick Road. The rest of the District needed its own schools because it was bursting at the seams with, for example, 1780 students in 1950, well over the 1948 projection of 1,200.

R. J. Lockhart
(Courtesy of the Massapequa Post)

Leading the movement toward a larger District was Raymond J. Lockhart, who was very familiar with student populations. Lockhart had been the first male Principal of the Massapequas (Massapequa School in 1930), and had overseen its expansion. In 1949, as District Principal (the Supervisor title came in 1955, when Massapequa's student enrollment reached 5,000), he proposed construction of a "new 15 classroom building to accommodate 450 elementary (Kindergarten through Sixth Grade) pupils and located in the northern part of the district ... at a cost of $850,000." The school, built on Baltimore Avenue and Broadway, was originally named Parkside, but was renamed **J. Lewis Ames** School in 1970. It was expanded and used as a junior high school in 1955. It barely made a dent in the problem, however, because the District enrolled 2,000 students for the 1952 – 53 school year. Students needed to be housed in temporary locations, and expedients were used: the Manor House, formerly George Stanton Floyd-Jones's estate known as Sewan was used, as was the Hicksville Road firehouse, Grace Church and the Mole Ford 10 car garage facility in Amityville, the latter for Kindergartners.

The District had adopted a policy of being one school behind, the better to convince residents of the need to pay for new schools. Despite opening **Unqua** and **East Lake** schools in 1953, the District could not and would not get ahead of the problem. Both buildings were Class 3 construction, meaning they were built of wood, which was cheaper and allowed faster construction. Students remembered the smell of fresh polyurethane and how the fields were seas of mud because the District didn't have the luxury of time to grow grass. At its peak, and after several expansions, Unqua School housed 1,500 students. In the accompanying picture, note the headline: "Overcrowding Moves East."

Unqua Dedication
(Courtesy of the Massapequa Post)

1954 saw the construction of Hawthorn School and provided another stark example of what was happening to the Massapequas at this time. There was an airfield in the middle of Massapequa Park named Fitzmaurice Flying Field, named for James Fitzmaurice, the first aviator who flew east to west from Europe to North America in 1928. Fitzmaurice Field opened in 1931 amid great fanfare, as an attraction for residents who owned private planes. They could land, take off and store their planes close to their homes and use them for business and/or pleasure. The Field had a small runway (1800 feet) and was never used heavily, especially during World War II, as fuel became scarce. It was used after 1945 as a training facility, operated by Tom Murphy, son of the original owner, and a location for stunt pilots, trained by Tom Tyler, a noted movie stunt man.

By 1952, District 23 was looking for any open spaces on which to build schools. Most space was gobbled up by builders, who were putting up houses at a frantic pace. Fitzmaurice Field was an appropriate target, so the Board approached Murphy, the owner, and offered him $600,000 for the property. Murphy was unenthusiastic, but realized he wasn't making much money as a flight trainer and could face the possibility of eminent domain proceedings, whereby New York State could take his property for a greater good (and schools were clearly the greater good). He therefore sold the Field in May 1953 and **Hawthorn School** opened in 1954 at the south end of the property. **McKenna School** opened four years later at the north end of the field.

Fitzmaurice Flying Field

People were settling all over the Massapequas, as can be seen by the locations of the new schools: **Parkside** and later **Lockhart** north of Sunrise Highway near Broadway, **Unqua** on Unqua Road between Sunrise Highway and Merrick Road, **East Lake** in east central Massapequa Park and nearby **Hawthorn**, in the center of Massapequa Park. **Birch Lane**, south of Merrick Road, was completed in 1956. All were grammar schools, but it was clear that a High School was needed, to accommodate graduates of **Parkside Junior High**. Massapequa students had gone to Amityville High School for many decades, but the Amityville School District balked about continuing to admit a growing number of Massapequans. There was no other nearby high school in the area, because neighboring communities were struggling with their population growth and were also opening high schools: Wantagh in 1954, Seaford in 1956, Plainedge in 1958. Amityville High School had existed since 1881, but it became too small to accommodate the influx of Massapequa students. The Amityville School District's message was that the time had come for Massapequa to build its own high school.

There were 7,500 students in District 23 by 1955 and they were all getting older! A high school seemed inevitable, and here again the influence of the Floyd-Jones family in Massapequa's history was evident. Sewan, George Stanton Floyd-Jones's mansion, sat on a slight rise on the north side of Merrick Road, east of Tryon Hall and west of Unqua. Floyd-Jones was a wealthy insurance executive, Treasurer of the Atlantic Mutual Insurance Company and active in civic affairs. He had, for example, opposed the Massapequa Water District's attempt to include his and adjacent property in their area of responsibility in 1930.

By that date George Stanton Floyd-Jones had become a convert to Roman Catholicism and a regular churchgoer. He lived a long life (1848 – 1941) and, upon his death, gave Sewan to the Sisters of Charity, who opened Queen of the Rosary Academy. It remained a Catholic School until 1954 (some public school students attended classes there) when the District bought the property for a high school. Sewan was torn down and a new building was completed, rated Class 1 because of its steel construction, in contrast to most of the elementary schools, which were cheaper wood construction Class 3 buildings. The school held eighty classrooms on three floors, including a gym and library and was filled immediately, to the extent that there was no room for a large cafeteria. Students then as now were allowed to leave the building for lunch.

New schools continued to open at a dizzying rate: **Carman's Road** and **Birch Lane began** in 1956, known as sister schools because of their similar construction pattern. **Birch Lane** provides an excellent insight into the population growth: it was a few blocks south of Merrick Road, in an area that was at ground level and subject to flooding from South Oyster Bay. Builders who saw proximity to the water as a lucrative attraction began to fill in the area, using sand dredged from South Oyster Bay in a process called hydraulic fill. They laid out streets and dug foundations, creating a new community that needed a nearby school. To drive home this point, the second public library, Bar Harbour, was completed in 1965, one block west of Birch Lane and designed to serve residents south of Sunrise Highway.

School Leadership

To complete the list, **McKenna Junior High School** was opened in 1958 on the northern end of Fitzmaurice Field. **Berner** opened in 1962, as a Junior and Senior High School, designed to absorb the relentless flow of students through the school system. **Berner** was built on Carman Mill Road, in the eastern part of Oyster Bay, on low land to the east of a creek that was originally the source of power for Carman's Mill, which stood on the site until 1911.The fact that **Berner** remained a high school until 1987 shows both how large the enrollment was and how it tailed off in the 1980s, allowing the District to redefine it as a Junior High.

Raymond Lockhart was well-known and respected within the school community because of his long involvement, beginning with his employment as the first male teacher at Massapequa School in the late 1920s. But it was an outsider with little educational experience who steered the District's growth in its early years. Alfred G. Berner was a banker who had moved to the Massapequas in 1929, when Queens Land and Title Company was building houses near Hicksville Road. His house on Seaview Avenue stood just south of Sunrise Highway and west of the Massapequa Preserve. He became involved in the school system in 1945, as a member of the Board of Education and as President in 1950. He was instrumental in the plans for the first several schools, overcoming the objections of taxpayers who were concerned over building costs by using wood instead of steel, which was more expensive and in short supply because of the Korean War, for construction. His influence was shorter than might be expected because he resigned in 1954 from the Board, citing business pressures. In fact, he had been ill for some time with a lung condition and died July 7, 1955 after a lung operation. He was 53 years old.

Berner Family
(Courtesy of the Massapequa Post)

The central focus shifted to Raymond Lockhart, serving as the District Principal. He continued the vigorous construction schedule Berner and he had designed, resulting in eleven schools, including two high schools, by 1962. Lewis Ames, elected School Board President in 1958, buttressed Lockhart's leadership, the latter having been named Superintendent of the enlarged District in 1955 and leading it until his retirement in 1966. A 1960 enrollment tally and projection provided by the Board of Education shows how necessary such a rapid pace of construction was:

YEAR	STUDENTS
1945	490
1950	1,780
1951	4,000
1958	12,446
1964	16,046
1970	16,237

The District naturally needed teachers for the onslaught of students and recruited them aggressively. There were 10 teachers in 1940 and 40 teachers by 1945. A long-time beloved teacher and administrator, Wilma Diehl, was hired in 1948 at $2400. In 1952 the starting salary was $3000 and in 1959 it was $4600. Candidates were often hired after a very brief interview with whichever administrator was available. Herbert Pluschau, long time teacher and administrator, remembered that many teachers were hired as temporaries or substitutes until time could be spared to observe them and assess their teaching skills. Many observations were never conducted, however, because of work pressures, and temporary teachers often were given permanent assignments because they had experience and were known by the staff. The 1964 student body was taught by 883 teachers, an astounding increase in fewer than twenty years.

1970 is considered the high point of Massapequa's population explosion. Most houses were completed by that time and the school population, over 16,000, started to decline, down to 10,566 in 1980 and 7,000 by 1985. The number of teachers dropped from 807 in 1970 to 681 in 1980. Both declines continued as the overall population aged and fewer new residents with young children settled in the area.

Population change forced revisions to the school system. **Berner** was downgraded to a Junior High School in 1987 and **McKenna** was transformed into a seventh grade center. **Ames** closed in 1987, but reopened in 2002 as a freshman school. The District faced continuing challenges to adapt its resources toward the end of the twentieth century.

In the spring of 1968, as a result of the recently-passed Taylor Law, Massapequa's teachers held an election to determine what, if any, organization would become the bargaining agent with the School District. The teachers overwhelmingly selected a local affiliate of the American Federation of Teachers, a national teachers' union. The organization was named the Massapequa Federation of Teachers, Local 1442. The President at that time was Harry Wilson, an English teacher at Massapequa High School. From that point forward, the MFT and representatives of the School District have negotiated a series of collective bargaining agreements (contracts) to define issues such as salary and working conditions.

In the early years, contracts were only one year in duration. In time, both sides realized the value of multi-year agreements that for the most part have resulted in peaceful relations between the parties. On occasion, however, negotiations were difficult and job actions resulted. In May 1970 the teachers went on strike for eleven days. Under the terms of the Taylor Law, those teachers who struck were penalized by losing two days pay for each day on strike, and President Harry Wilson and Vice President Robert Brooks served time in the Nassau County jail. Again in the early 1980s and mid 1990s prolonged negotiations led to months of picketing, accompanied by newspaper ads and public forums at which community residents often, but not always, spoke in support of their childrens' teachers.

As the years passed, the clerical staff of the District voted to join the MFT and today the union is known as the Massapequa Federation of Teachers (A Union of Teachers and Secretaries).

LIBRARIES

School systems and communities in general need to have libraries. The first large public library was Boston's, opened to the public in 1854. Public libraries have become common in the United States since the 1890s, when Andrew Carnegie became known for his generous support of libraries, starting in his home town of Pittsburgh and spreading throughout the Unites States. It is estimated that by 1930, half of all American libraries had been built by Carnegie.

In smaller communities, libraries were begun by individuals or civic minded groups interested in providing a place for reading, book borrowing, public meetings, or private reflection. Such was the case in the Massapequas, when in 1896 Delancey Floyd-Jones received a grant of land from his cousin Coleman Williams to build the library that bears his name on Merrick Road across from Cedar Shore Drive. The building had one reading room with books, shelves, and a center desk for the Librarian and visitors, and a small unfinished storage room in the back. It could accommodate 10 people comfortably and had about 6,000 books by the end of World War II.

Floyd-Jones Library
(Courtesy of the Floyd-Jones library)

Newly settled residents sought a variety of services in their community. As the school system developed, there were many discussions about creating a library system to meet the needs of children and their parents. The Floyd-Jones Library remained the only library in the area, but ironically had curtailed its hours to as few as eight per week as Floyd-Jones family members either left the area or became unavailable to serve as librarians. The President of the School Board, Alfred Berner, recommended a public library be created to meet the needs of a growing student body and community. A committee was formed in 1952 to oversee the creation of a public system, which included a review of the status of the current library. Among the options were to retain the Library as it was, namely as a private corporation, or to incorporate it into the public system through dissolution of its charter. Significantly, there was no mention of demolishing the building and replacing it with one or several larger libraries. In hindsight, that proved to be a unique and admirable position in view of the destruction of so many older buildings and artifacts in the Massapequas, and throughout Long Island.

The original title of the group was the Floyd-Jones Memorial Library Committee. After several meetings, members felt it necessary to separate themselves from the Floyd-Jones appellation, and designated themselves as the Massapequa Public Library Committee. This suggests their sense that their system would either be separate or would incorporate the Floyd-Jones Library into the public structure.

At the same time, Floyd-Jones Library Trustees held several meetings to decide how their status might be affected by the creation of a public system. Letters were exchanged and meetings were held with the Public Library Committee, correspondence was sent to the New York Secretary of State regarding the Library's Charter, and legal opinions were expressed about the possibility of two separate libraries existing in the same School District, each eligible for state funding. At one point, surprisingly, the Floyd-Jones Trustees indicated a willingness to give up their Charter and become part of the public system, but this never happened. It became apparent that dissolution would be complicated and expensive and that the public system would then gain control over the Library's endowment. Floyd-Jones Library

Trustees agreed ultimately to forego financial support from New York State, which allowed the public library to be created and the existing library to remain as an independent entity. The Floyd-Jones Library continued to operate separately along with the Central Avenue and Bar Harbour libraries, and patrons continued to use its services. It became less and less visited, however, as the new public library system grew.

A 1952 decision of the school board created a public library system, with an initial budget of $10,000 and a temporary location on the corner of Pennsylvania and Central Avenues. Some insight into the need for a larger building than the Floyd-Jones Library can be gained from statistics provided by Virginia Moran, Chief Librarian at the time. The temporary Library, housed in a store on Broadway, had by 1956 5,000 registered borrowers and circulated over 600 books and magazines a day. The permanent library, under construction, would have stacks for 25,000 books and a children's section that could seat 50 children and hold 9,000 books. By contrast, the Floyd-Jones Library had a collection of 6,000 books and could seat only 10 people comfortably.

The first of the two library buildings opened in 1956 on Central Avenue, on land donated by the Smith family. This initial building served new residents in the northern part of the Massapequas, but it became apparent very quickly that a second location was needed to serve the rapidly growing area south of Sunrise Highway. The Library purchased a mobile book trailer in 1961, making materials more available to the entire community, but this functioned as a stop gap measure.

In 1959 the Bar Harbour Shopping Center donated a parcel of land on the west side of Harbor Lane, allowing the School District to build a second library. The Library Trustees submitted a request for a bond issue to finance the new building. Surprisingly, the request was defeated by 156 votes, forcing the Board to rethink its strategies. After extensive discussions, several community meetings, and a professional marketing campaign, voters approved the new library in October 1963. Called the Bar Harbour Library, it opened in 1965, perfectly timed to serve the community that had developed around it (e.g., New Harbour Green, Biltmore Shores, Nassau Shores and Arlyn Oaks).

As the public library system developed, the Floyd-Jones Library continued to operate separately and patrons continued to use its services.

The library's activities can be gauged by reviewing a card file from the 1960s and 1970s which contains the names of several hundred students, whose parents signed an agreement permitting them to use the library, and accepting responsibility for the timely and safe return of books.

The Floyd-Jones Library faced new challenges in the 70s as fewer and fewer users visited. The modern and up-to-date public system attracted many residents, as had been expected. A Friends of the Library group was formed in the 1970s, growing to almost 200 members, to raise money through fund drives, bake sales, tours, and other activities, to meet continuing expenses. These efforts had a positive short-term effect, but were not continued. By the mid 1980s the library was barely kept open, and was no longer receiving books from New York State. Louisa Floyd-Jones Bonner, the last Floyd-Jones family member attached to the Library, resigned as Board Chair in 1985 and the Library fell into disuse and disrepair. Fortunately, Eugene Bryson, a long-time Massapequa resident and an Elder with Grace Church, accepted the position of Board Chairman. He supervised its physical renovation, including designing a second book room in the rear, hired a librarian to refresh the collection, and had the building repurposed as a historic building. His efforts breathed new life into a structure that remains an important part of Massapequa's past.

RELIGIOUS WORSHIP SITES

Protestant Churches:

It would appear that there was only one church in the Massapequas at the end of World War II, namely Grace Episcopal Church on Merrick Road, which had celebrated its one hundredth birthday in 1944. Strictly, St. Christopher's Chapel (named such in 1953) was affiliated with Old Grace, but it had long ago called its own pastor and had its own leaders. There was, in fact, a second church in the area, and that was the Christian Science Church created on Merrick Road across from Massapequa Lake in 1931. The church had taken over a real estate building established by the Fox Frankel Corporation, which was constructing and marketing Spanish-style houses in Biltmore Shores south of Merrick Road. It built a red brick building to house an office, meeting hall and reading room and remained active until 2007.

To muddy the waters about the first churches in the Massapequas still further, mention needs to be made of a church built in 1873, but not a part of Massapequa's history until 1947. The Bellport Methodist Church was constructed in the earlier year and stood on Brown's Lane and Maple Street. In 1945 the expanding Methodist congregation moved into a nearby Presbyterian Church, and the Brooklyn-Long Island Methodist Council informed local Methodists the Bellport church was available, if it could be moved. Local Methodists, who had held their services in the Massapequa Fire Department and the American Legion Hall, raised the funds needed for the tricky journey. The 26 by 44 foot church was moved off its foundation, placed on greased wooden skids and rolled one mile down to Great South Bay. It was then put on a barge and floated to Jones Creek, to be unloaded. Timing is everything, however, as the barge stuck in the mud by the shore (today's Burns Park) for six hours, until the tide rose enough for workers to transfer the building onto a truck for the half-mile trip to its current location. The 18 foot steeple was detached and shipped separately, to minimize interference with wires and trees.

AT THE END OF A THIRTY-FIVE-MILE VOYAGE

Methodist Church at Burns Park
(Courtesy of the Massapequa Post)

The site chosen by the Methodist congregation had its own important history. It was, for many years, the site of the only school building, a one-room and, after 1910, two-room schoolhouse used by students from 1870 until 1925. For the subsequent twenty years, the building was used as a utility and storage site by the District. Massapequa Methodists bought the site for $2,500 and contracted with the Kicherer firm to take down the old school, dig out a basement and lay a new foundation. Once that was completed, the building was moved to the site and set east to west, with the entrance facing Park Boulevard. It was named **Community Methodist Church.**

Anybody who visits the site today, however, would be confused because the church runs north to south, paralleling Park Boulevard, with the altar on the south side. The reason is another example of the enormous growth of the Massapequas in the 1950s. By the end of the decade, the congregation had grown to 1,500 members, far too large for the small church. As happened with so many other churches, Community United Methodist set the wheels in motion to build a larger structure, raising funds from the congregation and the community and breaking ground in 1961. One year later a new sanctuary, meeting hall and Sunday School were completed, in front of the original church and facing north to south. The original church, known among old-time members as the "Bellport Church," became a meeting hall and retains that function today.

The church developed an admirable reputation for challenging existing prejudices by inviting black residents from East Massapequa to worship and by appointing Rev. McQuay Kiah as its first black Assistant Pastor. Some residents objected to this challenge to the status quo, burning a cross on one member's lawn, throwing rocks through windows of other members, and writing racist slurs on their cars. Despite, or perhaps because of this, the church flourished, filling its new sanctuary and its meeting hall, which was the original "Bellport Church," for many years.

As the Community United Methodist Church grew, other Protestant churches were forming north of Sunrise Highway. In early 1950, Daniel Lehman, a Lutheran who had recently moved into the area, approached the United Lutheran Synod of New York about beginning a church. In June of that year the Synod created **St. David's Lutheran Church.** A pastor was assigned in 1950 and services were held in Massapequa Park's Village Hall. About 70 members attended Sunday Services and there were about 20 students in the Sunday School. As the Village Hall became too crowded (members had to stand outside and listen to the service), services were moved to Parkside (later Ames) School. In early 1952 the congregation purchased lots on the corner of Lakeshore Drive and Clark Boulevard for $11,800. Subsequent fund raising activities provided enough money for a church building to be completed in February. Prior to that, Sunday School was conducted in a doctor's office on Park Boulevard. Choir rehearsal was in a private house and meetings were held in the parsonage. Once the church was completed, and new residents moved into the area, membership continued to grow, reaching 587 by July 1955, with a Sunday School enrollment of 650.

As population growth continued, the original church became too small and a building campaign was started to build a new church and connect it with the existing structure. The new building, costing $300,000 was completed in 1960 and would serve a congregation that by then had grown to slightly over 2,000, with a Sunday School serving 1,000 students. As with so many other "traditional" churches, attendance began to decline by the mid 1980s, stabilizing at 1,500 people.

These two churches set the pattern followed by many others in the Massapequas. The **First Baptist Church** opened in 1951 at 89 Parkhill Avenue at the corner of Hicksville Road. The building was expanded in 1960 with the assistance of the Pastor, Harry Hobart, who did much of the carpentry, while other volunteers used their electrical and plumbing skills to save costs. The church had a small congregation at that time – 40 parishoners – so they needed to tap into their talents to build a permanent structure. Pastor Hobart estimated the total cost to be $40,000, a small amount at the time and astonishingly small from our current vantage point.

The Presbyterian denomination brought an unusual history to the establishment of the **Presbyterian Community Church** on Pittsburgh Avenue. There was a small Presbyterian Church located on Parkhill Avenue, but it closed in the late 1930s, and the building eventually came to house the Massapequa Republican Club. After the war, many new residents approached the Brooklyn-Nassau Presbytery about creating a new church. A meeting at the American Legion in July 1950 identified 28 members. They were recognized by the Presbytery and began to hold services, first in a small church on Broadway and later at the adjacent Parkside (later Ames) School. In September 1951 a Sunday School was organized and 100 students registered. As the congregation grew, its leaders sought out land for a church complex. They bought several parcels on Pittsburgh Avenue and built a Fellowship Hall and a Sunday School. In 1956 a capital plan was devised and a building fund was established, leading to $165,000 in pledges for a church building. Construction began in early 1961 and the Sanctuary was completed in September of that year. The Sunday School reached an enrollment of 1,000 students by the late 1960s. A Nursery School was established in 1958 and continues to this day, providing needed funds to maintain a church complex that now serves fewer members than at any time in its recent history.

A small unpretentious church was built in the middle of Massapequa Park to provide worship space for members of the Nazarene denomination, who had moved either to the Massapequas or to adjacent communities. A lot on the corner of Roosevelt Avenue and Wilson Street was purchased and the leadership of the New York **Church of the Nazarene** set about attracting a congregation and raising funds. The first service was held October 2, 1952 in Massapequa Park Village Hall with 136 in attendance. Subsequent services were held there and at East Lake School, where a Sunday School was also established. By 1956 enough money was available to build a wood-framed church, and construction began under the direction of Rev. Ralph Montemuro. The first service at the Church of the Nazarene was held on June 6 in a building that included a sanctuary for 100 members, a Sunday School room, a small apartment, a kitchen, restrooms, and a small nursery room.

The congregation continued to grow and a plot of land adjacent to the original church was purchased in 1972. Eleven years later the new, larger church was built and included a fellowship room in the basement. It also contained air conditioning, making it difficult for members to claim it was uncomfortable to attend services in the summer months! Reverends Ann and Anderson Rearick led the church through the 80s.

The **Massapequa Reformed Church** on Ocean Avenue and Merrick Road was formed later than the other Protestant churches. Starting in 1962, worshipers began to hold services in Unqua School and then in the American Legion Hall. In the latter instance, members replaced the picture of President John Kennedy with that of Jesus during services. In 1963 the Fraser property just north of Merrick Road was purchased and used as a church, school, meeting hall and social center. The building was designated as a church in 1964, to serve the 99 members. By 1966 that number had grown to 200, and they purchased the lot adjacent to the Fraser house, completing a new church building to seat 198 attendees by 1968. Funds came from members, other Reformed Churches, and donors who supported the new church. The Fraser house was subsequently refitted as a pre-school, a completely different sequence from the other worship sites, where the school preceded the church building. The Massapequa Reformed Church was the last to be built in this area in the heady days after World War II.

Roman Catholic Parishes:

Many new Massapequans were Catholic and they soon realized there was no Catholic Church in the area. The Catholics who lived in the area before 1945 would have attended either St. Martin of Tours Church in Amityville (1897), or St. William the Abbot Church in Seaford (1928). The Brooklyn Diocese originally served Long Island, but a separate Diocese was created in 1957 and installed at Rockville Center. Its leader, Bishop Walter Kellenberg, recognized the explosive growth of the Massapequas as well as other Long Island communities and moved quickly to provide structures for **St. Rose of Lima Church**, established in 1952.

Holland House

The parish encompassed 1900 families and Masses were held in the former Wagon Wheel Restaurant on Merrick Road, which was originally a Floyd-Jones mansion dating back to the late 1800s and known then as Holland House. It was redesigned to hold 600 worshippers, and around 1,700 members attended its four Masses on Sundays. Diocesan leaders gave priority to education and built a school to the east of the temporary church, opening it in 1960 for grades 1 through 6 (expanded to eight grades in 1963). Shortly thereafter, ground was broken for a church to serve the more than 2500 families. It was completed in 1965 and blessed by Bishop Kellenberg.

The geography of the Massapequas made St. Rose of Lima somewhat inconvenient for the many Catholics who settled north of Sunrise Highway and throughout Massapequa Park. **Our Lady of Lourdes Church** was thus begun in 1955. The emphasis in this area was also on education, as a cornerstone for what became Our Lady of Lourdes School was laid in 1961 off Carman's Road, just south of the Southern State Parkway. The property was a six acre farm owned by Michael Forte, who sold it, a farmhouse and three buildings in 1956 to what was then still the Brooklyn diocese. One building was used as a rectory, one as a convent, one as a chapel, and the farmhouse as a school until the new building was completed. Church services were held at Hawthorn, Carman's Road and East Lake Schools for many years. Surprisingly, Our Lady of Lourdes Church was not completed until 1985, by which time the school was well established and was drawing students from the Massapequas, Amityville and Farmingdale.

The Old Barn

... becomes THE FIRST CHAPEL

Our Lady of Lourdes Chapel

In her comprehensive and insightful book, <u>Richly Blessed. The Diocese of Rockvlle Center, 1957 – 1990</u>, Sister Joan de Lourdes Leonard lists 48 churches established throughout Long Island between 1945 and 1972. Along with two in the Massapequas, churches were also established in Seaford (St. James in 1951 and Maria Regina in 1955) and Wantagh (St. Frances de Chantal in 1952), underscoring population growth, especially of Catholics, along the South Shore. Cardinal Spellman, head of the New York Archdiocese, was responsible for breaking off the Rockville Center diocese from the Brooklyn diocese and for appointing Bishop Kellenberg, who was perfectly suited to lead it. According to Sr. Leonard, "Bishop

Kellenberg had gotten special training in insurance, real estate, and business administration, so he was given a diocese characterized by suburban sprawl and unrelenting physical expansion with its consequent building needs."

Jewish Temples:

Two temples served as worship centers for the Jewish community in the Massapequas. The first was Temple Judea, begun by members who began meeting in the back of Bob Mann's Shoe Store on Broadway in 1951. They later used the Community Methodist Church, Grace Episcopal Church and the Hicksville Road Firehouse for worship services. Like most other religious organizations, their primary focus was on education, as seen by the chronology of using Grace Church for its first school of 103 students and later using public school facilities. Known originally as the Massapequa Jewish Center, its members opened an eight-room schoolhouse on Jerusalem Avenue in 1955 and followed that by a Temple building in 1962. The congregation changed its name to Temple Judea in 1970 and continued as an independent organization until 2007, when it affiliated with the Suburban Temple of Wantagh to create Temple B'nai Torah. This procedure followed a common recent pattern among Jewish worship sites: two or more merging into one because of the dwindling numbers of congregants. This process was ably documented by Rhoda Miller in The Jewish Community of Long Island.

The other worship site was Temple Sinai, a Reform temple located on Clocks Boulevard down by South Oyster Bay. It was formed in 1958 and attracted Jews south of Sunrise Highway.

Statistics bear out the expansion and contraction of the Jewish population in the Massapequas, as well as throughout Nassau County. From only 17,300 in 1940, the Jewish population expanded to 155,000 in 1950, 345,000 in 1960, 372,000 in 1970 and 395,000 in 1980. The percentage of Jews in Nassau County jumped from 3.7% in 1940 to 23% in 1950 and a high of 29.8% in 1980. The Ku Klux Klan had made its presence on Long Island known between the wars, but Nazi Germany's defeat emboldened Jews from New York City to move eastward. Many had lived on the Lower East Side, a crowded and aging neighborhood that no longer attracted a younger generation. Smaller numbers emigrated from the central Bronx, and from Brooklyn and Queens.

The downward trend then began in the 1980s, from a population of 311,000 in Nassau County in 1990 to 207,000 in 1998, the last date for which figures are available. This led to the closure and/or merger of many worship sites A similar pattern was uncovered with other churches and in School District 23.

SHOPPING CENTERS

Shopping centers are built to serve a large population in a concentrated area. The Massapequas did not have a center for many years because the population was small and diffuse. In the late 1930s, however, it became evident that a concentration of shops in one area would be useful. The location chosen was along Merrick Road, just west of Hicksville Road, well-traveled thoroughfares that were convenient for residents throughout the area. It was also designed to lure residents of the recently-laid-out Shoreville Park community, south of Merrick Road. A large (at that time) building was completed on the north side of Merrick Road in 1938 and divided into six stores, which made shopping convenient for the few people who lived there. The stores were located to the right of Panchard's, a large white building that was a popular hotel and entertainment center from the 1920s until it burned in 1952.

Most shoppers on or around Sunrise Highway would have gone to the few stores along Broadway in Massapequa. The first store in Massapequa Park was opened on Park Boulevard in 1938. It served as a combination grocery store and post office, and was altered over the years as more stores opened in the late 40s and 50s.

The Bar Harbour Shopping Center was a much larger facility, reflecting the rapid population increase of the post-war period. It too was sited on Merrick Road, east of Harbor Lane and across from the recently-opened High School. Its location recognized the development of housing units in older areas such as Harbour Green and Biltmore Shores, as well as newer developments such as Arlyn Oaks and Birch Lane. The **Birch Lane School** opened in 1955 as residents moved into areas closer to the south shore and developers filled in the shoreline, extending it several blocks to provide a new network of streets with water-related names, moving from Atwater, to Highwater and Nearwater and ending at Tidewater and Waterview Avenues.

These new shoppers found a place to go in 1956 when Bar Harbour opened. It contained a Saks 5th Avenue store and Food Fair as "anchors" and 30 original merchants. Restaurants, shoe stores, a supermarket, clothing stores, household goods and athletic equipment were among the products offered. The shopping center had a large, immediate and continuing clientele from the High School across Merrick Road. Opened in 1955, Massapequa High School had a small cafeteria, but allowed students to leave the school for lunch. They naturally gravitated to the Shopping Center, where there were delicatessens and pizzerias serving quick and inexpensive lunches.

Bar Harbour Shopping Center 1958

Bar Harbour changed over the years, eliminating several stores in order to enlarge its parking lot, adding a second floor on the east end for stores and a movie theater, and enclosing a corridor running behind the stores on the south side. The Harbour Green townhouse complex opened in 1980 between the shopping center and Birch Lane School, and the center's name changed to Southgate. The number of stores decreased, but it remained a magnet for local residents and especially for high school students.

Moving into the 1970s the Massapequas lacked a mall, a common site at many Nassau locations such as Valley Stream (Green Acres), Garden City (Roosevelt Field) and Hicksville (Broadway Commons). The issue was resolved in 1973 when the Sunrise Mall was opened in East Massapequa, north of Sunrise Highway, on ground that had belonged to New York Water Company and was a muddy, weed-infested area. Nassau and Suffolk County residents living along the south shore now had a large shopping area for their convenience.

THE FIRE DEPARTMENT

The Massapequa Fire Department's history spans the entire 20th century and its several expansions resulted from the growth of the Massapequas. A marker erected by the Historical Society on its one hundredth anniversary in 2010 memorialized the department. It was placed on the location of the first firehouse on Grand Avenue, which is today, ironically, the headquarters of the Massapequa Water District.

Massapequa's population was growing in the early years of the twentieth century, as farmers settled in the northwest, German immigrants built houses in what became Massapequa Park, and the Queens Land and Title Company unveiled its ambitious plan to build a new city of 10,000 residents around Jerusalem Avenue in the area between the Massapequa Preserve and Tackapausha Preserve. Private citizens as well as elected officials grew concerned about access to water, both for home and business consumption, and for fighting fires. Eight individuals got together in 1910 and agreed to form a volunteer fire department to protect the area. William Hoffmann was elected Chief, Christian Wentzler Assistant Chief, John Jones (descendant of

Thomas Jones, the original settler) was named Treasurer and Howard Collins was designated Secretary.

The first motorized truck was purchased in 1917. Water was drawn from the nearest available stream, or from the newly-completed reservoir east of Broadway and north of what is today Sunrise Highway. After World War I, it became clear to all that better water sources were needed, especially with the emergence of the real estate firm of Brady Cryan and Colleran, who planned to fill the area that is today Massapequa Park with private houses. Accordingly, in 1930 the Town of Oyster Bay created the Massapequa Water District and signed contracts to lay pipes and establish hydrants, ensuring a more effective response to local fires by the Department.

The first firehouse, from 1910, a wooden shed located on a Brooklyn Avenue farm, burned down, and was replaced by a more modern facility in 1917. As the population grew in the 1930s, the large station on Hicksville Road north of Sunrise Highway was designed and completed by 1940, to serve the residents who had settled there as well as the few who lived in Massapequa Park, most of them in houses north of Sunrise Highway. A second house, called the Park House because it was located in Massapequa Park opened on Front Street in 1953, on the site of the former Woodcastle Hotel, as private houses proliferated in Massapequa Park. The earlier efforts of Brady Cryan and Colleran to populate the area were continued by several builders, filling in the area north and south of Sunrise Highway, and forcing the closing of Fitzmaurice Flying Field.

The Park House was well positioned to handle fires to the east of Massapequa Preserve, but the last wave of large-scale building left many new residents far from either house. Through the 1950s developers built houses south of Merrick Road, adding to the few houses built by Fox-Frankel in the 20s at Biltmore Shores and the several houses that made up Harbour Green. There were also a few small cottages that were used as summer places by New York City residents, but these were soon hemmed in by the many houses built down by the water, which had became a highly desirable location. The third firehouse, on Merrick Road and East Shore Drive, was completed in 1963 to serve the south and southeastern part of the

Massapequas. Today, almost 300 volunteers work out of one of these three houses, and respond to 2,400 calls in a typical year, a far cry from the 10 to 15 volunteers who reacted to 6 to 10 calls in the first few years.

The Fire Department has always been a volunteer operation and there was never any movement to create either a Village or Town Department. Costs are covered by money from the County and Town, as well as property taxes and donations from residents who are contacted yearly by volunteers. This practice began in 1947, when the first solicitation was held.

Firefighters' Memorial

A unique memorial on Park Boulevard honors the Massapequa Fire Department. Its origin underscores the Department's history of service. In 1975 Maureen Hogan died at the young age of 21 from the effects of diabetes. Her parents, Sheila and Michael Hogan, were profoundly grateful for the service provided by Department members, who were called upon many times to render first aid or to transport her to local hospitals. After many discussions with local leaders, the Hogans' wish to have a memorial erected to honor the department was granted in 1978 by Massapequa Park Mayor Robert Thompson. Thompson chaired a meeting at which Village Trustees agreed to erect a bell tower on the plaza in front of the Massapequa Park train station. He said at the time "We are in agreement that a monument to honor the volunteer firefighters of the Massapequas, will be created and placed in the plaza of the new Long Island Railroad station at Massapequa Park."

The actual tower took several years to complete, as it was done while the Long Island Railroad was elevating the Massapequa Park station. The Bell Tower Monument was finally dedicated on June 14, 1986. It was designed to remind viewers of the Fire Department's activities, but also to provide a repository of material from the period, to be opened one hundred years later. Several capsules within the Tower contain notes and letters, recordings about the area, records of events in the Massapequas' history, photo albums, telephone directories, currency, in short, a broad glimpse of life in this area in 1986.

The Tower was designed by the Serra Architectural firm and is topped by a bronze bell weighing almost a ton suspended 45 feet above the parking plaza. A circular inscription band, 12 feet above the base, unites the four pillars of the community and is inscribed "Massapequa Community Spirit 1981 – Honoring Volunteer Firefighters." The four pillars were designed to represent

The people of the community.
Professionals and Services.
Business, Industry and Merchants.
Government and Law Administration.

The circular pedestal base is made of granite, 20 feet in diameter and supporting the 55 foot steel superstructure. Four shafts of light from the center of the inscription band illuminate the bell at night and spotlight the bronze plaque covering the time capsule embedded in the base.

The Fire Department has a long and significant history, but the same cannot be said about a local police department because one was never created. Police services were provided by Nassau County from its earliest creation in 1899 and that tradition continued after 1945. There were sporadic discussions among the Trustees in the Town of Oyster Bay and the Village of Massapequa Park, but there was never a concerted effort to create a separate force. Residents have for many years received police services from Nassau County's Seventh Precinct, located on Merrick Road in Seaford.

THE WATER DEPARTMENT

Fire Department members were always conscious of the need to have ready access to water. From its earliest years, the Department was able to pump water from streams and lakes, or from the reservoir created north of the railroad tracks and in the middle of the Massapequa Preserve. This was one of several reservoirs created along the south shore in the 1890s to provide water to Brooklyn and later to Queens. Nassau County water was pumped into the Ridgewood Reservoir and drawn out by city residents. After 1918 it became evident that Massapequans needed their own dedicated water source. Accordingly, the Water District, founded in 1930, reached an agreement with the New York City Water Service Corporation to take control of its reservoir, as did the other towns along the south shore.

The 1965 – 66 drought was the last episode in the conflict over control over Nassau County's water. The County allowed New York City to tap water from Queens and Brooklyn for several months. The Water District finally gained control over the former Brooklyn system in the early 1980s. In July 1981 Nassau County bought 1,750 acres of watershed land, including the Massapequa Reservoir and all of the Massapequa Preserve, from New York City, for $6.7 million. The remainder of the original Brooklyn property was purchased in June 1986.

The original customer base in 1930 was 672 residents, living at 184 sites. By 1955 the Water Commission was servicing 9,090 connections, requiring miles of transmission pipes and eventually 9 pumping stations. The number of connections reached 13,000 by 1985 and service was provided to 40,000 residents. Five wells were dug between 1954 and 1957, three along Ocean Avenue and two along Hicksville Road. The enormous growth of the Water District in the post-war period underscores sharply the unprecedented growth of the Massapequas during this period.

Because of strong opposition in the late 1920s from George Stanton Floyd-Jones, who owned Sewan, and Louise Floyd-Jones Thorn, who owned Little Unqua, the southeastern part of the Massapequas was not incorporated in the water district, and is today served by Aqua Water. Further, the area north of Jerusalem Avenue is serviced by the Farmingdale Water District, using lines laid originally in the 1920s.

GOING TO THE MOVIES

After new residents bought their houses, sent their children to schools, located libraries and used them for books and research, selected places of worship and found stores for their shopping needs, they looked for entertainment sources. It's revealing to note that for many years any resident wishing to go to indoor movies would need to travel outside Massapequa (as they need to do today!). The *Massapequa Post* in 1955 advertised movies showing in Amityville, Merrick and Farmingdale, but none in the Massapequas. The first indoor theater was created in September 1960 on the second floor of the newly-opened **Bar Harbour** Shopping Center (today Southgate Shopping Center). The first feature was *The Mouse That Roared*, shown on a wide screen with air conditioning. The theater became known as an art house, showing specialized films for several weeks in a row. A biography of Sigmund Freud, for example, was featured in spring 1963. The theater lasted until 1980, when the Southgate Apartments were built and the shopping center was redesigned with fewer stores. The theater was subdivided into several businesses, which continue to occupy the space today.

The **Pequa Theater** opened in 1964 on Sunrise Highway east of Broadway. It featured an all-glass lobby and exposed ceiling joists, and showed adult themed first run movies. *To Kill a Mockingbird*, for example, had a long run in the spring of 1963. Long-time residents remember that it was a very comfortable theater with good sight lines and acoustics. It closed later than the **Bar Harbour Theater**, lasting until 1989, when it was purchased by a car company. The Datsun Motor Company (later changed to Nissan) bought the site and it is today a Nissan and Infiniti dealership.

There was also a **small theater in North Massapequa**, housed in the shopping center located today at the northwest corner of Jerusalem Avenue and Hicksville Road. It opened in October 1960 and closed in the late 1970s. It was located on the first floor of a two-story building, with a Fred Astaire Dance Studio on the second floor. Patrons remembered being distracted by the dancing, especially the tap classes. Little else is known about the theater. A Marshall's Store now occupies the site.

An additional theater existed for a brief period in the shopping center on Carman's Road across from Our Lady of Lourdes Church, in the extreme northeast of the Massapequas. Very little is known about it except that it was small, plain, and not well-maintained.

One of the most unique theaters built in the entire Long Island area was the **Jerry Lewis Theater**, opened in December 1972, on the site of a former drive-in. *Love At First Bite* was the first showing. Jerry Lewis was an enormously popular entertainer in the 1950s, with his partner Dean Martin. Their television shows achieved the highest ratings and helped bring television sets into most American households. After the duo broke up in 1956, Martin went on to make several crime-related movies, while Lewis became a star in many comedies. In 1966 he became director of the Labor Day weekend telethon to raise money for Muscular Dystrophy research and treatment.

In 1970 Lewis coordinated with the Network Cinema Corporation to open a chain of theaters across the country. These would be small, with about 200 seats, technologically sophisticated so they could be run by as few as two people, showing second run family run movies, and charging low admission prices to attract families. Franchises could manage their own theater after paying $15,000 to $50,000 as a down payment. Network Cinema Corporation would provide name recognition, as well as marketing and technical support. Three others were located on Long Island, in East Meadow, Lake Ronkonkoma, and Center Moriches.

The Jerry Lewis enterprise can best be described as quixotic. There was little advertising or oversight of each theater, so it was left to the franchisee to sink or swim. Most franchisees had little knowledge about operating movie theaters, and the initiative was overwhelmed by the development of multiple cinema sites, which became very popular starting in the late 1970s. The Jerry Lewis Theater chain sank very quickly, including Massapequa's theater, which closed in 1980. The building subsequently housed several businesses and is today a Staples store in the rear of the Phillips Shopping Center. Of the 130 theaters in the Jerry Lewis chain nationally, 12 are still open, under different names. There are none in the New York area.

Drive-In Advertisement
(Courtesy of the Massapequa Post)

The **Jerry Lewis Theater** replaced the first theater in the Massapequas, the **Massapequa Drive-In**, which opened in 1952 to the rear of what was first Frank Buck's Zoo and later became the much smaller Grimaldi's Kiddie World. The Grimaldi family sold the rear of their property to the Prudential Cinema Company, which opened a one-screen drive-in. It was one of many drive-ins that opened after the war across the country. Several others on Long Island included those in Valley Stream, Bay Shore, Westbury, and Huntington. They were very popular with families and with teenagers (for reasons that won't be discussed here).

The **Massapequa Drive-In** showed double features, such as *From Here to Eternity* and *The Solid Gold Cadillac* in June 1960. It was usually opened in the warmer months, but there are advertisements in the *Massapequa Post* about shows in the winter (*Quo Vadis* in January 1965, for example). It also showed horror films, with *The Day of the Triffids* an especially creepy offering as day turned to night. The Massapequa site felt the same pressure as other drive-in locations as the population grew and demands for houses and stores increased. It lasted until 1968, about the time most private houses were completed nearby. It represented an ideal site for a shopping center, on Sunrise Highway with ample parking. The theater closed shortly after Grimaldi's Kiddie World and the site reopened as the Phillips Shopping Center.

All indoor theaters described above were small, most with one screen, but the 1970s saw the growth of cinemas with many screens, typically five to ten, offering a wide variety of choices. One of these was the **Multiplex at Sunrise Mall**. The Mall opened in 1973 and the theater in 1976, operated by United Artists. There were five screens at the beginning. Two were added in 1979. Entry was originally on the first floor, but the box office was moved in the early 90s to the second floor, in the center of the mall. Although very popular in the beginning, the site suffered declining attendance through a combination of vandalism and the development of the Farmingdale Tenplex, a few miles north on Route 110. The theaters closed at the end of their lease in 1999 and are now the sites of several stores.

THE LAST BIG THING

The enormous changes that occurred in the Massapequas might have spurred a long-time resident to ask "when will it ever end?" A helpful answer would be 1981, when the last major change to the Massapequas took place, namely the elevation of the Massapequa Park railroad station. All other stations along the Babylon branch were elevated by 1975 (including Massapequa in 1953). There was a small wooden waiting room at ground level, and riders had grown accustomed to waiting there or in the open for trains to arrive. That may have accommodated the few residents of "the Park" in 1940 (488), but population growth again forced change. From 2,334 in 1950, Massapequa Park's population shot to 19,904 in 1960 and 22,112 in 1970, before leveling back to 19,779 in 1980.

Maʃʃapequa Park Station 1940

The enormous 753% increase in the 1950s earned the Village the distinction of being the fastest growing municipality in the United States. Ridership increased proportionately because many new homeowners worked in New York City. The platforms were raised in the 1960s for safety purposes and to accommodate newer trains that rode higher on the rails, but the ground level crossing was a constant danger, prompting continuous letters to editors, and editorials calling for an elevated station. The Metropolitan Transportation Administration had taken over the Long Island Railroad in 1970, and its leaders were willing to consider an elevated station, as Village officials had begun to suggest. There had been eleven fatalities attributed to the level grade crossing and train drivers were instructed to slow down when approaching Massapequa Park. The Village attempted to alert people by sounding a loud and piercing horn every time a train approached. After a brief period of time, residents became aggravated by the sound of the horn, going off at all hours of the day and night.

By 1973 talks had progressed among the MTA, Massapequa Park and New York State sufficiently to allow the *Massapequa Post* to boast in a May 17, 1973 editorial that work would begin on the structure in twelve to eighteen months. That prediction proved overly optimistic because wrangling over details and costs postponed plans from being drawn up until January 1976, when the engineering firm of Charles Sills submitted detailed drawings of the new structure, and the necessary detours that would be required to facilitate the work. Sunrise Highway would need to be detoured further south, resulting in elimination of the center median and the road shrinking to two lanes in each direction. Discussions went on continually over the placement of drains, electrical cables, and new roadways, and over the quality of the material used in the construction. In fact, the original cement used to cast the structure proved to be defective and needed to be recast. The additional work in this case was performed at the Kicherer Yard, a large vacant lot across Sunrise Highway from Sunrise Mall (52 East Chestnut Street) named after the Kicherer family, multi-generational Massapequa residents who laid the foundations for many of the houses built in the area.

Robert Thompson was Village Mayor during this period, and insisted in maintaining as much control of the process as possible. He fought with both the MTA and New York State over payments, and insisted on maintaining control over the station, including its maintenance and appearance. The Massapequa Park station, for example, is one of the very few on the LIRR that controls its own advertising. Thompson was also worried about the price tag. Original estimates put the total cost of elevating the station at $12 million. The final cost was $35 million. It's remarkable that work was completed at all because New York City was going through a fiscal crisis and the subway system, which was part of the MTA, was in disastrously bad condition. The winter of 1980 – 81, for example, was statistically the worst in the system's history, using MDBF (Mean Distance Between Failures) numbers, as well as other commonly accepted measurements.

Massapequa Park Station Supports 1978

Despite these negative forces, the station was completed to the point that it was formally dedicated on December 18, 1980, with final completion scheduled for 1981. By the end of that year, Massapequa residents had witnessed the last of the major changes that led to the area looking as it does today.

V. FRANK BUCK'S ZOO

The Frank Buck Zoo was one of the most unusual features of Massapequa's life in the mid 20th century. It was located on Sunrise Highway across from today's Sunrise Mall, lasted from 1934 to 1965, and is one more illustration of the drastic changes that occurred in the area after 1945.

The zoo was the brainchild of famed wildlife hunter Frank Buck, whose slogan was "bring 'em back alive." Buck, born in Texas in 1884, became a big game hunter in the 1920s, captured animals in Africa, and insisted on keeping them alive for zoos and other locations. He provided many species to the Bronx Zoo, and gained a reputation as a hunter who cared for and protected his animals. He created and operated a large exhibit at the Chicago World's Fair in 1933, and established zoos in his native town of Gainesville, Texas as well as in Massapequa.

Buck chose Massapequa because he felt it was an ideal location: near New York City, with railroads and recently opened Sunrise Highway, and undergoing population growth. He learned of a 20 acre site developed by Charles Beall, a banker who wanted to exhibit animals, but lacked the capital to do more than build several animal houses. Buck signed a 10 year lease in 1934 for Beall's site and stocked it with a large menagerie: lions, tigers, leopards, elephants, hippos, rhinos, giraffes, antelopes, zebras, snakes, birds, and, most popularly monkeys, who were exhibited on a 100 foot monkey mountain. He had up to 500 monkeys and they caused him the most trouble, escaping several times. The largest escape occurred in August 1935, when over 100 got out and ran loose through the Massapequas for several days.

Buck's Zoo was popular until World War II, but then suffered from restrictions common throughout the country. Gasoline was rationed, so people couldn't travel by cars. Railroad travel was also discouraged because of the need to preserve fuel for the war. It became increasingly difficult to procure meat for the big cats, fruit for the smaller animals, and hay for the elephants. Many young men, some married, went off to war, depleting an important segment of the population. Buck lost interest in the zoo during the war, spending more time near his Gainsville, Texas zoo, closer to his home. The Massapequa location was taken over in 1944 as an arms plant, operated by the Cochran Manufacturing Company. It was not a government defense plant, but was responsible for supplying cartridges and bullets for police departments and other groups whose ammunition supplies were restricted by the war. About 100 workers would typically repair spent shells and bullets and refill them with gunpowder and primers for later use.

Buck and his partner, T. A. Loveland, shipped most of the animals to other zoos around the country, and allowed the site to languish for a few years after the war. Buck was seriously injured in a 1947 auto accident, and remained in ill health until his death in 1950. The Grimaldi family, who lived in the Massapequas, bought the front part of the property and reopened it on a smaller scale, aiming it at younger children. It was variously titled "Sunrise Kiddieland," "Sunrise Kiddieland and Animal Farm" and, finally, "Massapequa Zoo and Kiddie Park." Several smaller animals were enclosed in a petting zoo, including a buffalo, llamas, deer, red foxes, African sheep, exotic birds, and domestic farm animals. One long-time resident who worked there recalls he was responsible for caring for a bear, walking the animal and showering him in the hot weather.

The Grimaldis added a carousel, jet plane, boat, and fire engine rides, as well as games of skill and chance. They had success with their enterprise, but rising land values and the development of other attractions led them to close the park in 1965. The Phillips Shopping Center now stands where the zoo was located. The only remaining building is the lion house, which is now a fitness center.

VI. Saving the Past:
Old Grace Church and
the Historical Society

Amid all these dramatic changes described above, Old Grace Church endured as the oldest place of worship in the area, celebrating its 100th anniversary in 1944. It too soon felt the pressure of growth, as it became far too small for the growing population. It was built as the Floyd-Jones summer church and expanded in 1905, but could hold only about one hundred worshippers. Active membership of 145 worshippers was documented in 1939. By the mid 1950s it was too small for the growing congregation, so its Vestry members followed the typical pattern of raising funds, buying property, and designing a larger church to meet parishoners' needs. A lot directly across Merrick Road, that had been donated to the church by John D. Jones in 1880, and was farmed by, among others, the Kicherer family, was purchased, and the "new" Grace Church was constructed, opening in 1962, for a congregation that had grown to over 3,000 by then. Appropriately, a small Floyd-Jones mansion dating back to the 1880s existed on the property and was turned so it faced the church. It had been converted into a rectory in the 1890s for long-time rector Reverend William Wiley and continued to be used for that purpose. In contrast to other churches, the school (Grace Church Day School) was built later, in 1963, and would be used for many years as the main school building. Prior to its completion, kindergarten classes were held in the Floyd-Jones house.

The new church was far larger, and the older building came to be used less and less. In summer 1969, it was vandalized on two different occasions, raising concerns about its security. The Church's Vestry decided to use Old Grace sparingly, usually on large feasts, or for special ceremonies (e.g. Baptisms) at the request of its members. Vestments, chalices, candles and other liturgical artifacts were brought across from the new church for services, which became less frequent through the 1970s. As an old building, it needed continuing maintenance, which inevitably raised the issue of its function. Father John Jobson had become rector in 1974, and questioned whether it was time to take down the building. He and the Vestry felt maintaining the property would be a significant and potentially crippling continuing expense.

Their review of Old Grace's status alarmed many congregants as well as community members, and revived a small organization that had received a charter in 1969 for its concerns regarding church vandalism. On two occasions during the summer of 1969, youngsters had broken into the church, damaging brass fixtures and the altar rail, emptying fire extinguishers on pews and the organ, and damaging woodwork. A small group of residents, notably Anne Markiewicz and Lorraine Newman, were alarmed by the 1969 vandalism and formed the Massapequa Historical Society. They held several meetings with Assemblyman Philip Healey, leading to his granting of a provisional charter to the organization.

Anne Markiewicz and Assemblyman Philip Healey
(Courtesy of the Massapequa Post)

As there were no further incidents of vandalism in the 70s, the Society became inactive, but it revived in 1980 to face the possibility that Old Grace would be destroyed. Anne Markiewicz deserves great credit for arranging public meetings, typically held at Marjorie Post Park, for organizing a Preservation Festival in October 1980, and for leading discussions with Father Jobson and the Vestry. Historical Society members and Anne were concerned that the destruction of Old Grace Church would be one more example of the willingness throughout Long Island, and Massapequa especially, to destroy history in the name of progress.

During the 1945 – 85 period, seven mansions built by the Jones and Floyd-Jones families were destroyed and there were very few buildings in the Massapequas still standing that were built before 1900. Old Grace was the best known of these "old" buildings, so it became a powerful focal point of the need to preserve Massapequa's history. Discussions went on for several months, with church leadership remaining firm in its apparent resolve to destroy the building, to the point that Father Jobson set May 15, 1981 as the date to begin demolition. He and the other Vestry members held off, however, in the face of growing community opposition as well as unease within church membership, many of whom were baptized, married, and attended services regularly in the historic building. Finally, in August 1981, the Vestry agreed to lease the church to the Historical Society for 25 years for the sum of $10. Grace Church was thus relieved of the need to maintain a decaying building and the Historical Society took on the task of rehabilitating it.

Save Old Grace Church

The Historical Society became a large and vibrant organization as a result of its "Save Old Grace" campaign. Anne Markiewicz indicated there were 107 Society members in the middle of 1980. That number grew to over 500 by 1981, to 700 members by 1990 and over 1,000 by 2003. It set about the task of repairing the church, most notably locating stained glass windows from St James Episcopal Church in Delaware, New Jersey that fit closely. The windows in Old Grace had been removed in the late 1970s and placed behind the altar in the new church. The old building was then boarded up. The Historical Society raised funds to have the substitute windows resized and installed in 1985. It also reinstalled the window behind the altar, as well as the altar rail and the missal stand, which were removed by the Grace Church Vestry. It then improved the heating system, repaired the belfry and modernized some of the electrical system. Support for these projects was provided by several generous donors: The Beato Fuel Oil Company provided a new heating system, Kaplan Brothers donated lumber, labor unions contributed their skills at the request of Assemblyman Philip Healey, local engineers and lawyers provided free advice and guidance.

In order to raise money for these projects, the Historical Society charged membership fees and began to have outdoor festivals: Preservathons in 1980 and 1981, a Strawberry Festival in June and an Apple Festival in October. An organizational structure was developed, with a President, Vice Presidents, Treasurer, and Trustees to direct its activities. It subsequently (1986) oversaw the move of a Servants' Cottage that was part of Elbert Floyd-Jones's estate on Merrick Road and Park Boulevard, across Merrick Road to its current location, just to the east of Old Grace Church. These buildings, along with the 1896 Floyd-Jones Library, came to be called Massapequa's Historic Complex, and were identified as such by a historical marker erected in 2011. The Society can truly be said to be an organization created by the ferment that embroiled the Massapequas in the postwar period.

The Historical Society has also become the central repository and reminder of Massapequa's history. It possesses a large and comprehensive collection of documents, newspaper articles, photos, and artifacts that illuminate our past. Importantly, it has erected sixteen historical markers throughout the Massapequas to remind residents of what was here. Much of the credit for that initiative belongs to Arlene Goodenough, President on two occasions in the 1980s. In 1985 she spearheaded a campaign to have a historical marker placed at the entrance of Jones Beach, recognizing Thomas Jones as the first European settler of this area. Subsequent markers have highlighted many of the features described in this book: the Fire Department, Fitzmaurice Flying Field, the Fort Neck Mansion, Massapequa Manor, the Fairfield School, Frank Buck's Zoo, and indeed the Historic Complex itself, a central location for grasping the history of the Massapequas.

Thomas Jones Marker 1985

The first marker provided by the Historical Society is also the only one not located in the Massapequas, and is not a large blue and white sign anchored on a metal pole at its appropriate site. The Thomas Jones marker is set in the cement on the south side of the Jones Beach traffic circle around the water tower. It was put there because the Historical Society wanted to emphasize that Thomas Jones owned the beach as well as the area north of South Oyster Bay. The marker reads

MAJOR THOMAS JONES
Born in Ireland c. 1665
Died 1713. Buried in Massapequa
Settled in Fort Neck. Now Massapequa
In 1696 with wife Freelove Townsend.
Owned 6000 acres on Long Island
Established a whaling station
On this beach.

---

*From distant lands to
This wild waste he came
This seat he chose and
There he fixed his name
Long may his sons this
Peaceful spot enjoy
And no ill fate his
Offspring here annoy*

HISTORICAL SOCIETY OF THE MASSAPEQUAS

As an aside, the Historical Society is formally titled **The Historical Society of the Massapequas**. Several members in the early 1980s objected to the original title of "Massapequa Historical Society" because it ignored the diversity of the area: sections such as North Massapequa and East Massapequa as well as the incorporated village of Massapequa Park. Ira Cahn, founder and publisher of the *Massapequa Post*, championed the name change. The Trustees resolved the issue nicely by defining their organization as The Historical Society **of the Massapequas.**

68

VII. THE VIEW FROM 1985

1985 seems an appropriate date to close this review of the history of the Massapequas (with a bit of spillover to 1986) because of several revealing events of that year. The Historical Society was able to save the Floyd-Jones Servants' Cottage, and to raise the money to move it from behind the Bar Harbour Public Library to its current location in Massapequa's Historic Complex. The Historical Society was also able to find appropriate stained glass windows and have them installed in Old Grace Church, completing the major project of saving and reviving the landmark building. The Historical Society further began the continuing process of erecting markers on historic sites, placing one in the pavement at the entrance to Jones Beach to commemorate Thomas Jones' settlement along the Massapequa River.

At the same time, the Kiwanis International Club undertook the task of moving one of Fred Stone's log cabins from its site in East Massapequa to Burns Park, dismantling it piece by piece, numbering each piece and reassembling it at the southeast corner of the park, where it is used by the Boy Scouts, and as a storage facility for the Town of Oyster Bay.

1985 also was the time when the Fire Department memorial was approved. It was erected the following year, as discussed above.

At the same time, Massapequa and its adjacent communities experienced downward movements in the 1980s. The population of Oyster Bay skyrocketed during the 1945 – 80 period:

1940 – 42,594
1950 – 66,930
1960 – 290,055

1970 – 333,342

By 1985, the population had dropped to 305,750. Similar retrenchments occurred in the school population (17,000 in 1970, 10,566 in 1980), leading to the closure of the Ames campus and repurposing of Berner as a Junior High School. The numbers of worshippers in several religious sites also declined, with Grace Church membership declining from 2,310 in 1968 to 1,251 by 1992. Subsequent years would see a continuing "churn" as older residents moved or passed away, and younger people purchased existing houses. The great upheaval caused by the post-war rush to Long Island was replaced by a slower and steadier population exchange.

VIII. CONCLUSION:
A SETTLED SUBURB

There are two ways of looking at Massapequa's history since 1945. The first would be to imagine our veteran going to sleep one evening after searching for a house in the area. He was twice as tired as Rip Van Winkle, so he slept for forty years, instead of twenty. If he awoke in 1985 and walked along Merrick Road, he would have noticed the disappearance of all the imposing mansions that he saw in 1945. Moving eastward,

> The Red House, by then a small shopping center east of Seaford Avenue and the grounds part of Tackapausha Preserve;
> Massapequa Manor, east of Massapequa Lake, the site of many private houses;
> Holland House, later the Wagon Wheel Restaurant, the site of St. Rose of Lima Church and School;
> Sedgmore, later the Oddie House, occupied by private houses across from St. Rose's;
> Sewan, now Massapequa High School;
> Unqua, the site of a shopping center, today anchored by Ace Hardware;
> Little Unqua, now used for recreation as Marjorie Post Community Park;
> Kaycroft, location of Parkview Nursing Home.

Let's look realistically at our returning veteran. If he had moved into the Massapequas in the early 1950s, he would now be in his sixties. He would have had children, and they would have gone through the public school system, or one of the private schools in the area. He may have worshipped at one or several of the churches that were founded after the war. He could attend meetings at the American Legion Hall or the Veterans of Foreign Wars Hall. He could have become involved in the Kiwanis Club, the Knights of Columbus, the Ancient Order of Hibernians, or the Knights of Pythias, or other service organizations. His wife may have joined the Massapequa Garden Club or the Fort Neck Garden Club. She would have shopped in one of many stores along Broadway in Massapequa/North Massapequa, or Park Boulevard in Massapequa Park, or in stores along Merrick Road or Sunrise Highway. More conveniently, more stores became concentrated in the Bar Harbour Shopping Center in the mid 50s and in Sunrise Mall after 1973

The 1950s homeowner's children could play in Brady Park after 1957, Mansfield Park by the 1960s or Burns Park by the 1980s. The entire family could attend one of the six movie theaters that sprang up at this time. In the summers, the homeowner could go with his family to Tobay Beach or to Florence Beach, or, if they preferred a pool, to Marjorie Post Park, for swimming, picnicking, ball playing, walking, or playground use. In the forty years since the war's end, he would have been in the center of a whirlwind of change, growth, and development.

Along with many other long-time residents, our veteran might decide to retire and resettle, typically to Florida, Arizona, or other warm weather areas where there were fewer people, and the costs of living were significantly lower. Although social planners have for decades decried the difficulties associated with living in such a high cost area, the original houses bought by returning service people and others in the 50s have always sold very easily to younger generations, who moved from the New York City area, convinced the Massapequas provided a good location to raise children as well as a convenient commute to the city. They would compete for housing with other home buyers who were the children of the original settlers, who enjoyed growing up in the "Pequas", and wanted their children to enjoy the same conditions they had experienced.

Residents who moved to the Massapequas after 1985 would have experienced none of the enormous changes that took place before their arrival. This book is presented for them and for all who lived here, or who are interested in the history of suburbia, as a reminder of the earth-shattering and multi-faceted changes that occurred as Massapequa and the United States became suburbanized.

IX. REMINISCENCES

Everybody carries memories of their early lives and remembers events that are significant to them. Residents who grew up in the Massapequas shared these memories:

Swimming in the beach at the end of Alhambra Road. It was clean and well-maintained and many youngsters learned to swim there, because the water was calm and shallow. The American Red Cross gave swimming lessons in the summers.

Working at Grimaldi's (originally Frank Buck's Zoo) and tending to the bear that lived there. Activities involved feeding the bear, walking him, and showering him in hot weather. Fortunately, the bear and his teenage handler got along very well.

Changing schools constantly in the early 1950s: sessions were held in the old Floyd-Jones mansion, at Mole Auto Annex, in Grace Church, at the firehouse and almost anywhere that would accommodate students.

Berner was built as a High School in 1962 and retained that level until 1987. One woman remembers meeting her husband at a fair behind Bar Harbour held at the 60th anniversary of the Fire Department. He was wearing a Berner High School jacket and represented "the enemy." When he visited her, he was required by her brothers who attended Massapequa High School to leave his jacket on a railing on the stoop of her house. He could come in, but not the jacket.

Berries were an important feature of the Massapequas for the earlier settlers. One long-time resident remembers picking grapes from the Massapequa Preserve and bringing them home for her mother to make jam. Another remembers picking blackberries from a field across from Fairfield School in the later 1950s. Still another picked blueberries from fields around her house in East Massapequa.

All American Hamburgers, opened in 1955, was considered an unsafe place for teenage girls. That was where the "bad" boys hung out. Girls were told by their parents to stay away from there. It will not be disclosed here whether that advice was heeded.

One woman who moved here in 1973 bought a house built in the 1920s that had a coal bin with a door on the outer wall that allowed delivery to be made from a coal scuttle.

Father John O'Halloran, Massapequa's historian in the 1950s, remembered seeing a shell heap left by Native Americans at Clinton Place, near Ocean Avenue. Known as a midden, this remnant of long-gone settlers was only visible at low tide.

The Floyd-Jones Servants' Cottage was originally named the Coachman's Cottage. It was occupied by the man who drove Elbert Floyd-Jones, and later his wife Elizabeth, in their carriage before automobiles. It was renamed the Servants' Cottage in the 1980s, with one Floyd-Jones family member insisting that it be clearly titled to show it was a cottage for her family's servants.

A long-time teacher remembers moving to the area near the Bar Harbour Library in the 1970s. He remembers when the aging Floyd-Jones Servants' Cottage was in its original location just north of the Library. To those who say it was unoccupied, he replies it was occupied regularly – by a family of raccoons.

Nancy Todaro moved to East Massapequa in the early 1960s. She remembers attending rallies and standing on picket lines with her mother Virginia, who was confused that East Massapequa had a different telephone exchange and zip code and was in a different school district (Amityville). Mrs. Todaro's work paid off and East Massapequa was moved to the 79 (Pyramid) telephone exchange and assigned zip code 11758, along with the rest of the Massapequas (except, of course, Massapequa Park, which has zip code 11762).

Floyd Kenyon was Principal of Birch Lane Grammar School from 1973 to 1984. He succeeded Ruth Young, who was the first Principal. She was very strict and the school was called the "most Catholic public school on Long Island," because of its reputation for strict discipline. Ironically, it was only learned recently that Floyd Kenyon was a descendant of the Floyd-Jones family. His mother was a Floyd-Jones, married a man named Kenyon and named her son Floyd Jones Kenyon. So there was a continuance of the Floyd-Jones influence into the 1980s, although very veiled.

A life-long resident remembers fires started in what is today Philip B. Healey Beach (previously Florence Avenue Beach). The area was swampy and full of bullrushes in the 1950s, and pranksters would start fires in the summers. The Fire Department was busy putting out these fires because houses had been built on nearby Florence Avenue by then. The area was converted to a family-style beach in the 1960s.

When the Bar Harbour Shopping Center was redesigned and renamed Southgate, a tunnel behind the buildings on the south side was filled in with concrete. Unfortunately, a car that was driven into the tunnel could not be started and was left there. Anybody who wants it may contact mall management.

Two residents remember attending the high school in May 1958 when one student murdered another in the building. Bruce Zator and Timothy Wall had argued over a girl several days previously. Zator was suspended, but entered the school on April 30 and shot Wall in a boys' bathroom. One Historical Society Trustee's brother witnessed the shooting. Zator was captured, pleaded guilty to manslaughter, and was sentenced to 10 to 20 years in prison at Elmira Correctional Facility. He died of cancer while in prison.

PRINTED SOURCES

Altschuler, Glenn C. and Stuart M. Blumin, <u>The GI Bill. A New Deal for Veterans</u>. New York: Oxford University Press, 2009.

Collora, Christopher M., <u>Long Island. Historic Houses of the South Shore</u>. Charleston, S. C.: Arcadia Publishing, 2013.

<u>Dolph's Atlas of Nassau County Long Island</u>. New York: Dolph and Stewart, n. d.

<u>Fifty Years of Memories</u>. The Community United Methodist Church, 1997, provided by the church.

Goodenough, Arlene, "The Baldwin-Hilbert House," <u>The Freeholder</u> (I: 1 Summer 1996), 1.

<u>The History of St. David's Lutheran Church in Massapequa Park, New York</u>, provided by the church.

Jackson, Kenneth J., <u>Crabgrass Frontier. The Suburbanization of the United States</u>. New York: Oxford University Press, 1985.

Kirchmann, George, <u>Signs of the Times</u>. Massapequa: 2014. Printed privately.

Leonard, Sister Joan de Lourdes, <u>Richly Blessed: The Diocese of Rockville Center, 1957 – 1990</u>. Marceline, MO: Walsworth Publishing Company, 1991.

<u>Long Island Almanac</u> (Ronkonkoma, NY: Long Island Business, 1997).

Massapequa Annual, 1955, 1958.

Mettler, Suzanne, Soldiers to Citizens. The GI Bill and the Making of the Greatest Generation. New York: Oxford University Press, 2005.

Miller, Rhoda, Jewish Community of Long Island. Charleston, SC: Arcadia Publishing, 2016.

Moran, Virginia, "Massapequa Public Library," Massapequas Annual, Fall 1956, 6.

Newman-Brooks, Lorraine, The Massapequas ... From the Time of the Native Americans to the Year 2000. Printed privately.

Our History: Massapequa Reformed Church, provided by the church.

Our Lady of Lourdes Parish History, provided by the parish.

Poliakoff, Ira, Synagogues of Long Island. New York: The History Press, 2017.

Smits, Edward J., Nassau. Suburbia USA. Garden City, NY: Doubleday & Co., 1974.

The Massapequa Post, An Illustrated History of Massapequa. Massapequa: Massapequa Publishing Co., Inc., 1968.

The Temple Judea Story, provided by the Temple.

Wiley, Ralph, Preacher's Son. New York: Vantage Press, 1972.

Winsche, Richard, "When Nassau Supplied Brooklyn's Water," 150 – 157 in Joann P. Krieg and Natalie A. Naylor, eds., Nassau County. From Rural Hinterland to Suburban Metropolis. Interlaken: Empire State Books, 2000.

In addition, this publication benefitted from the numerous articles written by Massapequa's long-time historian John H. Meyer.

INDEX

Printed and bound by PG in the USA